Special....and Then Some

Chronicles of a Political Grass Roots Journey

Maryellen Berryhill

published by Sarah Jane Berryhill

Contents

Copyright   8

Title Page   13

Chapter 2: Gathering Momentum   23

Chapter 3: Signage and Loyalties   26

Chapter 4: Supporters Are Golden   31

Chapter 5: I Did It My Way   35

Chapter 6: Post Primary   38

Chapter 7: Election Has Arrived   48

Chapter 8: Landslide Berryhill   54

Chapter 9: Special....and Then Some   60

Chapter 10: Serving   61

Chapter 11: Chaos moving into the Election   67

Chapter 12: The Aftermath   71

Part two: AND THEN SOME!   76

Chapter 1: It Begins..Again   77

Chapter 2: ...and....We're Rolling!   85

Chapter 3 Territory   89

Chapter 4 May events   94

Chapter 5 All Over the Map!   102

Chapter 6 The June 6th Primary   105

Chapter 7 Placer and Lassen Counties   108

Chapter 8 Placer County   113

Chapter 9 El Dorado and Tuolumne Counties   120

Chapter 10 Plumas County   124

Chapter 11 Tuolumne County and 'the Cabin'   127

Chapter 12 Georgetown and Amador County   132

Chapter 13 Lassen County   137

Chapter 14 Northern Counties, Alturas and Modoc   143

Chapter 15:   The Mountains of Placer, Amador &   154
Tuolumne Counties

Chapter 16: Amador, Calaveras, Placer County   157

Chapter 17: Calaveras, Amador and Stanislaus County   164

Chapter 18: Stanislaus and El Dorado County   169

Chapter 19: Stanislaus and Tuolumne County   176

Chapter 20 Seeing is Believing   179

Chapter 21 Election Night   185

Chapter 22: Decision Time 1976   187

FOREWORD

It is with great honor I was given the opportunity, after many many years, to bring my Mom's book into fruition, as she had requested so long ago. I don't think she had any idea how relevant her story sharing would be in this day and age where political honor and integrity were so in question as never before. It is time that we, as a country, wake up and pay attention!

The timing and an acquaintance of a new friend who was familiar with dad while he was Director of Agriculture for California, prompted me to get the book put together and "out there" to the public, given politics has gone somewhat sideways. Our representatives have become more committed to those that buy their election than to the constituents they represent. We need to remember that we vote them into office and they work for us, the American people. Holding office is supposed to be a role where an individual is employed by the people they are to represent. It's a rare bird, as my Mom would say, to find a politician with integrity, focused on really addressing the issues of the day without petty worthless bills that do nothing to improve our quality of life, serving only to distract and confuse the public while they go and work on bills that are not for our best interest but in theirs.

It is time to re-focus. It is time to wake up and pay attention. It is time to get back to real grass roots politics. It is time to pay attention to those running for office, discerning consistency and a hearts desire to help the American people create a more stable lifestyle, not just to pad their personal pocketbooks. I myself do not choose my candidate based on their party at this point in time. Party values have changed over time and have become too polarized for someone who is moderate. It used to be there was a level of cooperation between all parties, but you just don't see that today. When I pick a candidate, I look at their words versus their lifestyle, their promises versus what they have delivered in the past. I examine who they tend to vote with, what references they have, if they have heart. I look for consistencies — what a candidate said five years ago and what they are saying today. We all have the right to change our minds, but not to play games. There are many red flags if you are a constituent paying attention. Don't complain about who represents you if you aren't aware and attentive to who you have helped vote into office. We help vote people into office in many different ways; by not paying attention, by not helping or supporting the better candidate, one who votes with common sense and not necessarily on party lines, and often for not making the time to get to the polls to vote as well as help others get to the polls to vote. Every vote counts. Don't think in terms that your one vote does not — it does.

My Mom and Dad were both eternal optimists — you will pick up on that as you read. They believed if you could dream it and it created passion, then you could make it happen. Dream it, do it. All five of us kids caught that concept and we have all shot for the moon more than once! Sometimes it worked out, sometimes it didn't. What I also want to say is that it was not always easy being a child in this family. We had many adventures that were amazing beyond what most can imagine, but there was also a loneliness present as well. Not many could relate to your life and how you lived, and it was also apparent people believed everything they read or heard on the news – not really understanding how the system works and the games played behind the scenes – which is where the real agendas played out. You learned to just observe and have input when it seemed appropriate — not a bad habit I will add. Each of us had a different way of being, a different way of coping, a different way of expressing, and a different level of involvement.

I was the more reserved child in this family, so I learned to play guitar and write songs as my way of surviving what often felt like a mad dash to the finish line with elections ever present. Tom, Bill and Betsy were more involved in the political side, though we each threw our all into the process in action. The publishing of this book will be my way of putting the concepts we were raised with politically out into the world for others to contemplate.

Thank you for taking the time to read these adventures taken with our family along with the lessons we learned along the way. We five kids all grew up with deep awareness of how the system works and does not work, and with our individual perceptions.

Both of my brothers have been involved in California politics, following in the footsteps of my dad. Tom Berryhill has held the offices of both State Assemblymen and State Senator. My brother Bill served a term as a State Assemblyman and currently runs a wine business under Berryhill Family Vineyards (www.berryhillfamilyvineyards.com). Sister Lynne, Betsy and I are proud sisters, knowing that they served the people of their districts with heart. This is what we were taught, and this is our path, though we each went about serving the public in different ways.

Jane Berryhill

SPECIAL ELECTION 1969

Of all of the problems I conjured up of marrying a farmer, one I never anticipated was becoming involved in politics. Of all the activities discussed over a cup of coffee in our farm kitchen, the plotting of a political campaign was least likely.

Clare had always had a feel for the land and was a top operator in our special field of wine grapes, dehydrating fruit and growing diversified crops. I had known in my bones ever since I was a little girl that I wanted to marry a farmer and raise a big family. All of these things were mine, and I was so happy with our family of five children, 4-H activities, music, sports, friends and farming.

Hard work, far-sighted planning, and a good gambler's sense of timing had brought Clare to the point where he had reached his major goals in agriculture at the ripe old age of 35, and he had hit a period of restlessness.

Retire? Not likely. Buy more land? He had done that. We had scraped and borrowed and lived through many lean years to reach the present point. Should he sit back and watch the results of his labor and enjoy life? We had always been able to do that. In the worst years, developing the ranch, we had thoroughly loved our life, with the special richness of raising a family on a farm where roots are developed strong and deep.

During this time, we turned as always to God to direct our steps. "Not my will, but Thine be done." We knew that by following all of the human footsteps required and listening for the 'still, small voice', that proper guidance would appear. Whoever said that God works in strange and wonderful ways certainly had it figured out.

We were about to embark on a strange and wonderful path that led to a wholly new life, a different challenge for Clare, and for all of us as well.

Maryellen Berryhill

Chapter 1: A Family Affair
(or, decisions, decisions, decisions!)

Memory fails to record and keep many special things in politics as in all else, but there are some memories of the special election of 1969 that I don't want to lose for our family, or the many friends who worked so hard for Clare.

At stake was the 30th Assembly District seat in California, and the battle for control of the State Assembly by either the Republicans or the Democrats. Clare was a Republican.

A cold, heavy and unrelenting January tulle fog blanketed our farmhouse outside the farming town of Ceres, in Stanislaus County, which is in the heart of the rich San Joaquin Valley. The sun seemed to have deserted us and we were enduring our annual period of the depressing gray that settles upon us every year, broken only by hopping in the car and heading for the ski slopes, or perhaps for a picnic in the nearby foothills where we could look down upon the sea of fog that blanketed the valley below.

If our dining room table could talk, it could tell of other foggy January days when we sat alone or with friends sipping coffee, discussing last year's crops, optimistic about the coming year.

No matter how bad or how good, the gambling man who is the

farmer spends those dormant months anticipating the coming spring, and all of the things he is going to accomplish. This was also the time of year that we always bought additional property.

Some evenings we would venture out through the fog to visit friends or welcome them to our home, where a cheery fire and a glass of wine would always greet them.

Clare and I enjoyed people and lots of good conversation. In our circle of friends there were many hot and heavy discussions over politics, how to prune the grapes, the price of calves, or the local schools. I swear, there was never a time when anyone was caught without an opinion on any given subject or day.

My initiation into participating in the Republican Party was a bit of a shock. I was pregnant for the second time when a woman called me on the phone to ask if I'd help do precinct work. I said "Sure! We'll be glad to help." Little did I know that it would be the start of many happy years of grass root support for Republican candidates.

The caller was Carie Osterholm, rounding up volunteers. She wanted us to take 14 precincts. "Gee," I said, "I'd love to but I'm expecting my second child!"

"How do I get to your house?" she asked.

She drove out with a station wagon full of very small boys, and *she* was pregnant! She wore an over sized t-shirt that said "I like Ike." Down below that it said "Me too!"

While I tightly grasped my 18-month-old Betsy to my own rather obvious bulge trying to protest my predicament, my bulges didn't hold a candle to her carful! But it wasn't 14 precinct lists — it was 40!

Clare was a member of the local school board, active in service clubs, and had very strong political convictions. But Clare wasn't the first member of his family to get bit by the political bug. His great-great uncle was the renowned Charles Evan

Hughes Sr., the 44th United States Secretary of State as well as the 11th Chief Justice of the United States Supreme Court. Another member of his family who got involved in the political process was his grandfather [name], an attorney who fought Standard Oil of California all of the way to the Supreme Court. In the end he lost the battle over possession of Signal Hill in Southern California. But that's another story.

The particular foggy morning I am about to refer to found our good friend Rae Codoni sharing coffee with us as we reminisced over the events that had occurred since last November.

This was one of many mornings we shared with Rae. He and Clare got along well and had worked together closely with our local Growers Harvesting Committee in order to resolve labor problems in the area. Rae also had an interest in politics, having worked as campaign manager for three successful elections of his best friend, Jack Veneman, to the California Assembly. These campaigns started Republicans off to an imposing string of special election victories.

We had all worked for his election. Jack was a farm boy and, at the time, a good County Supervisor. We were, after all, living in the bread basket of the world.

We lived in a predominantly heavy Democrat district dominated by the liberal McClatchy newspaper, but we blithely went ahead and elected him anyways. The past November Jack had answered the call from then President Richard Nixon to go to Washington to serve as Under Secretary of Health, Education and Welfare to Robert Finch; Finch had left the post of Lieutenant Governor of California to take the top job. While the rumors were flying considering Jack's imminent appointment, the Democrats were getting in gear. They had never put up a strong candidate against Veneman, and even the McClatchy paper had come over to him, or visa versa. Now was their big opportunity to make a move.

A local attorney, Assistant District Attorney Ernest LaCoste, had been biding his time to break into politics, and this seemed made to order. He quietly began lining up support, capitalizing on the fact that many of the agriculture community who had supported Veneman were disenchanted with his increasingly liberal views. Constituents were also unhappy with his seemingly lack of communication in Sacramento as well as at home. LaCoste was busily selling himself as a farmer, having recently acquired a few acres of almonds, a beat-up pickup and casual shoes.

The Republicans were in a quandary. No clear-cut candidate appeared, and there was hesitancy about going with men who had been defeated in their quest for office in the past. It was with a great deal of surprise that we read in the evening paper, early in December 1968, that Jack Veneman was picking his successor for us. Ray Simon. Who was he?

A group of us were enjoying an evening with good friends from Modesto, Pat and Lowell Clark, when the conversation veered from Christmas shopping to politics. Lowell and Pat were also good friends of the Venemans. Lowell was an active community worker and had been urged in the past to run for office. Clare said, "How about it Lowell?"

While Lowell calmly sat puffing on his pipe, Clare continued. "You have the time now and we really need you. Look at the support you would have from all of us!" Lowell just shook his head and mentioned Ray Simon. Clare responded, "Ray Simon is an up-and-coming young City Councilman. With Jack's blessing and Ray's beautiful wife, he is looking awfully good."

Codoni spoke up, quietly. "What about someone who can represent agriculture?" Someone else piped up, "Okay, Rae, are you ready to go?" Rae sat back looking like he was the fellow who had just invented sliced bread. "Hell no," he said with a grin.

After a few moments of dead silence, everyone started talking at once. Rae threw Clare's name into the ring. "Politics is so rough on families," someone said, and in all sincerity, since our friends know how much we cherish our family life, and that Clare was so successful at this point in time. The group went on and on, with many more good and valid reasons why this was one of the worst ideas that Codoni had ever had!

Christmas and New Year's came and went before Jack's appointment was verified. We took the kids skiing for our annual vacation up to Tahoe. Politics lurked around every lift and filtered in and out of our conversations. Our five children were more attuned to politics than most, since they had accompanied me on precinct work since car seat days, as well has having a dad committed to serving local government on the school board for nine years.

The kids were developing faster than we realized, learning the lesson that this government needs local people actively striving for solutions to problems. What wasn't needed was more concerned people coming up with more problems. They had been active in going door-to-door for candidates Eisenhower, Nixon, Jack Veneman, and most recently Ronald Reagan, who was now Governor. They knew a bit about campaigning! They also had a little practical experience in the subject of economics, since Clare had always offered them the opportunity to work on the ranch to earn money for what they wanted. Child labor laws being as restrictive as they were, believe me, they knew how lucky they were to be able to earn money while their town friends were restricted from most jobs, by law.

Clare employed around 40 fruit cutters every summer in his dehydrator, and there was always a waiting list of students from high school wanting to be put on as a cutter. Since they can't start this work until sixteen years of age, the efficiency level left a lot to be desired.

Our own children started cutting fruit at age nine, standing on a lug box, so they were very proficient by sixteen! As the minimum age went up, and Pure Food and Drug laws became more restrictive, it eventually became financially impossible to continue cutting apricots. The kids rallied to the cause, formed their own informal corporation, bought apricots on the trees, cut them, bagged them, and sold enough to finance their skiing for two or three years. Clare stayed in the dried peaches and golden raisin business for several years more. It is a tough business, but one which financed the development of our farm, our primary goal.

One of our few fond memories of those dehydrator days is the day that Dick and Pat Nixon stopped with their entourage at the plant during a campaign swing through the county. Pat graciously walked through the wet and sticky dehydrator and spoke to all of the employees. We can't take full credit for the coup of stealing the candidate from the big city of Modesto to our little city of Ceres, however, but do give full credit to our courageous editor of the local newspaper. He was an old timer to politics, Maitland S. Pennington.

Mait had given up a much more lucrative job in Washington D.C. in the Maritime Commission to buy our local paper, the *Ceres Courier*. He had been a lifelong friend of Senator Tommy Kuchel, and their fathers had both been involved in the newspaper business. Mait was a tall, big man with light hair and bushy "John L. Lewis" eyebrows, with an impressive demeanor! He was deeply patriotic and had told us with great eloquence how much the United States of America had done for him. At the very time in his life when he might have started to relax his pace, he flipped a coin to decide which of two small-town newspapers he was going to buy. We won Mait, his wife Mary, and their two sons, Dallas and Dan. Mait's mother been a suffragette in Oakland and she was active in Earl Warren's first campaign. With this background, he had a great wealth of experience to bring to Ceres, and was a born raconteur. So it is little wonder that he convinced the Nixon entourage with his voice of authority — which he had developed over years of dealing with long shore men and politicians — that the real political plums were to be picked at the Ceres Dehydrator rather than the Modesto airport!

We were still suffering the January doldrums out at the ranch, and this particular morning with Rae and umpteen cups of coffee was no different than usual. We were still discussing politics and the progress LaCoste was making with the ranks of rural Stanislaus County. The likelihood of Ray Simon's candidacy was strengthened by Veneman and the commonly stressed view that the Republicans must have a candidate from Modesto where most of the voters resided. The point was also made that it should be a rather non-partisan type candidate.

The first fly-in-the-ointment was the development of still another candidate from the Republican ranks, the ex-mayor of Modesto, Pete Johansen. He was a better known person, but still did not reflect the agriculture background that the district needed. A very nice man, Pete didn't seem to have quite the aggressive personality to take on the tough fight against LaCoste.

As Clare and Rae kept rehashing all the points in the game, I retired to another room to ask once again for the guidance to do what was best for all of us. My personal wishes have always been so wrapped up in the "we" and completely oriented to Clare, myself and the kids, that to jump into something so alien to our private life was a tough prospect. But calmness came to me, giving me the reassurance I needed.

Rae was arguing that our family ought to come first. With tears in his eyes, he discussed the rough world of politics as he had experienced it. As he continued to speak, a resolve began to form in the expression on Clare's face, and it was now apparent to both of us.

Who knows what would have been the outcome if Simon or Johansen had come to Clare to get together on a candidate.

Instead, the Republican State Central Committee, stepping into the picture with a steering committee to assess the candidates, would decide for us who would be the best candidate. Word trickled down to us that we "lived on the wrong side of the river" and, therefore, Clare wouldn't be the best candidate. Veneman was mustering formidable support for his choice, Simon, among his buddies in the Assembly. Veneman's close friends, with the exception of Codoni, were rallying behind Simon. Another group, including at least one other former supporter of Jack, were publicly endorsing Pete Johansen.

Friends were in almost constant contact with us, urging Clare to run both for the sake of Agriculture and the Republican party and urging him NOT to run for the sake of his family. Our dining table was more like a verbal Ping Pong table than a place to eat!

Our close friend Dick Davey and his wife Marian had been among the most eloquent of those arguing for Clare to stay out of politics. Dick had been a coach, they had raised two fine children, and they were most concerned about Betsy, Tom, Lynne, Janie and Bill. We were all aware how blessed we were in the life we had at present, and we certainly didn't want to jeopardize their future. In this day and age, many youngsters don't have both parents at home, often both parents are working. We knew the pressures were simply too great on the children in these situations.

At this point I made up my mind. I'm fearful of a lot of things our bunch had done, such as climbing the barn roof, riding our ornery burro Banjo, or having dirt-clod fights. I knew without a doubt they had the background to make it, just as I would. It would be hardest on Tom and Lynne, eleven months apart and both in high school. Lynne would still have Tom, but Tom and his dad were very close and their separation would be hard to take. No one had ever accused me of being independent. We had to look upon it as an opportunity to grow and develop.

When Dick saw the resolve building, bless his heart, he agreed to be co-chairperson and formed the Berryhill Boosters Club, a group of loyal friends who would be the nucleus of Clair's support base. Fearing a very bad spot in the party, thus ensuring victory for LaCoste, Rae and Clare decided to visit Veneman in his Sacramento office and apprise him of the problems facing all of us as a result of Jack's hand-picking a candidate. If you want to stir up a hornet's nest, throw two old friends, one a stubborn Dutchman, the other a volatile Italian, add a frustrated, indignant Welshman, and STAND BACK!

For whatever his reasons, Jack refused to talk to them at all at first, but when they simply pushed into his office, he went over the problems not only with them but with a third party entering the conversation via the telephone. The gist of their talk was, "Clare can't win." They had the wrong Welshman. Clare's determination to become a candidate was growing stronger by the day, and the days were getting short for filing to run. He had never in his life turned down a challenge, especially (and usually) against rough odds, and he had never lost. This was an important facet in his personality that only his closest friends were aware of, as his acquaintances knew him mostly as a "nice guy," a "good buddy" and "lucky" farmer. I knew the other side and went through a great deal of mental anguish for him knowing how good he was to all of us, how he cherished and appreciated his life as it was, and yet I also knew he needed a new challenge.

Two things brought about the decision to become a candidate. First, the Stanislaus County Central Committee meeting that Clare was asked to attend. Also invited were Ray Simon and his campaign chairman along with Pete Johansen and his campaign chairman. Codoni was left out, which made us mad, although in all fairness Clare was not yet a declared candidate. Since this was not a meeting open to the public, not many people were aware what exactly transpired. But the local newspaper, the *Modesto Bee*, got wind of bits and pieces somehow and made quite a story about the secret meeting. We had a very bad taste in our mouths about the whole event. At the meeting, Clare got a lot off his chest about power politics, but agreed that if only one candidate filed he would not run. However, if Pete or anyone else DID file, then it was going to be a wide open primary, which is the way he thought it ought to be anyway. Then he turned on his heel and walked out of the room.

At home we had a family conference. Our children had quite a few opinions of their own and laid it on pretty thick. They told us how we had always taught them that it was important to get involved and fight for what you thought was right. I think they even threw in the bit about any poor kid having the opportunity to become President! Somehow, it all seemed a bit overly dramatic and unreal. We did get carried away with our own enthusiasm and decided, "Why not?" We knew we would always regret it if we didn't try, and Clare was positive that he could win the primary — no matter what anybody said.

Chapter 2: Gathering Momentum

This particular year our family consisted of eight people instead of seven. We had Betsy — who was in high school as a senior; Tom was a sophomore; Lynne a freshman; Janie in Junior High; and Bill in elementary school. In addition, we were host family to an AFS foreign exchange student from West Germany, Gaby Frenzel. Gaby considered herself an enlightened and progressive person — much more rational and objective than the rest of us! However, if her crazy American family wanted to give this a try, she wanted to be a part of it.

Growing up in post-war Germany, Gaby was vehemently anti-Nazi and pro-socialist. Within her frame of reference, when Gaby arrived at our house – all Republicans were equated with Nazis, and the press was much higher in her estimation than politicians. She really had to fight her convictions to muster enthusiasm. She said, "Dad, you just can't win if the party doesn't back you!" Dad said, "in this country, and especially in California, this just isn't true. People here vote more often for the person rather than the party. With a lot of help from our friends, we will show you how it's done!"

A few days later I called Gaby in to watch a press conference on television that Governor Reagan was conducting. This changed her attitude more than any other one thing. What she knew of the press and politicians in Germany simply wouldn't stand up to this free and open exchange between our Governor and our reporters. She became very indignant over what she, in her wisdom, considered asinine questions and Reagan's patience in answering more or less the same things over and over again. For a basically reserved girl, she became quite a Reagan and Berryhill fan. In all honesty, many other people shared her original concerns.

A few weeks earlier we had attended a State Chamber of Commerce dinner meeting in Sacramento with Sid and Linda Long, Ceres farm friends, to hear Professor S.I. Hayakawa speak about the student activist problem at the universities. We entered the hotel past a motley group of picketing folks carrying signs decrying Hayakawa. Many of the signs had been used before on behalf of Cesar Chavez, simply turned over, and the anger of the moment expressed on the opposite side. Of course they were all well-covered by television cameras and were featured prominently on the news the next day.

Before dinner we were chatting with old friends from the Modesto Irrigation District, both whom had been elected to the Board of Directors many times, and therefore had reason to believe that they knew more than a little about politics. One of them was expounding on the invincibility of Ernie LaCoste in the upcoming election, and how he would show those two Modesto politicians a thing or two! He mentioned the widespread support from the agriculture community for Ernie, and especially from republican farmers.

It got to be too thick for Sid. Grinning amiably, he leaned over and said in a friendly fashion, "We think we have a guy from agriculture, really from agriculture, that can take LaCoste." In pure disbelief, the man said, "Okay. There isn't anyone. Who could it be?" Sid just nodded Clare's way and said "If we can get him to run." As the implication sunk in, we turned our attention back to the speaker.

Our friend Sid made a few inquiries in the next few days and then called to chat with me. I couldn't say anything at that time, because we were not yet sure what we were going to do, so we just kept him guessing along with the rest.

On another evening we were going to a dinner in Turlock when Dr. Gerard DenDulk, our family physician, stopped by the house to go with us. He didn't know that Clare was even tinkering with the idea of running. He was talking about Ray Simon and his endorsement by Jack Veneman. Both the doctor and Jack were from the Dutch community in the valley, so I wasn't sure how he would take our attitude to the situation. However, if you can't talk to the man who delivered all five of your children, who can you talk to?

Only two or three close friends had been in on our discussions up to this point. I rode to Turlock with him, and as he quietly listened, I spilled all my pent-up feelings about Veneman, the State Central Committee and whatever happened to government "of, by, and for the people"? I don't know what all I said, but it sure felt good! He was off and running on our side from then on, and was a very strong influence in Ripon, his conservative Dutch hometown in San Joaquin County. He had a strong influence, as well, in the medical circle of doctors in Stanislaus County where he had practiced for many years.

The last day for filing arrived, and Clare was committed. We were ALL committed.

Chapter 3: Signage and Loyalties

Ernie LaCoste was so sure that Ray Simon would win the primary that he had billboards and brochures that said "Elect a Farmer" and showed old "Farmer Ern" leaning on a friend's tractor — wearing Hush Puppies.

I felt sorry for that friend because he was an old school chum of ours, too. Both Clare and Ernie had grown up in Stanislaus County, and I had lived all my school years in Modesto when it was such a small town that everyone knew everyone else. It was going to be tough on our mutual friends who wouldn't want to hurt either of their feelings. Many chose up sides, however, and it was our friends who helped run our headquarters, drummed up finances, and organized groups for Clare to meet.

Homer Vilas and his enthusiastic cheerleader personality pulled in many supporters from the Turlock area. Dick Davey approached Ceres and Modesto Democrats to convince them to join the team. George Ground called us one evening from a dinner party and volunteered his wife Edwina's services. We thought he had just gotten carried away, but lo and behold, the next morning, "Wina" breezed in the door, went to work, and was there when needed every since. Old friends and new friends all jumped in to help get things done. One of the best parts of campaigning is the gathering of friends, many of whom have gone their busy ways for years but are there when you need them.

One of the most hilarious campaign pranks involved a giant banner that said "BERRYHILL" and was to be pulled behind an airplane. Our high school band director and part-time flying instructor, Bert Stevenson, volunteered to tow said banner, but we were stymied by the "Silver Fox" Harry Sham, a very well-known and influential man in the field of aviation in the area. He was backing Pete Johansen, and also possessed the only towing hook up in the valley! Harry was a pilot from the early barnstorming days of aviation, an instructor, and was manager of the Modesto Airport. We had to get permission from Fresno for Bert to tow the banner, which was accomplished, but getting it away from Harry was something else!

I was so sorry that he was committed to Pete, but loved him and his wife Muriel, who had helped me cope with those original forty precincts as well as teaching me A LOT. The "Silver Fox," Harry, was so named for his beautiful head of hair, and his foxy way of collecting more money for candidates than anyone else. He was a formidable opponent. He had flown a similar banner for Joe Shell a few years before, and that's where we got the idea. Bert was as determined to get that banner up as Harry was to keep it down, and the tow in his keeping. First he flew out of town with it. Eventually, Bert got it, heaven only knows how. Up, up and away, as the song goes, and he soared over fields, highways, reservoirs, shopping centers, and wherever a crowd was gathered. Bert Stevenson got a big bang out of the whole thing!

Harry eventually flew a banner for Pete, too, but we got ours up and that's all we wanted.

The big billboard was another example of grassroots ingenuity. LaCoste seemed to have outclassed us in the number of billboards that popped up around the district. A group of Clare's supporters, mainly farmers from San Joaquin County, discovered a spot for a super billboard, bigger and higher than any candidate had ever had, in the town of Manteca.

At the old Celia winery property on the west side of Highway 99 stood a tall old water tower, situated at a curve in the highway where it can be seen for miles in either direction. If Bob Goodwin were still with us he could tell this tale better than I, but I'll do the best I can.

Bob was a local grape grower in Manteca, who was an active member of his community, had an amiable personality and a home filled with warmth. He agreed to be campaign chairman for Manteca, which took a load off of our minds. When the group of growers put their minds to the problem of getting signs up on both sides of that gigantic tower, there was no stopping them.

The difficulty in raising and positioning two billboards so high off of the ground was a tactical problem of no small magnitude, and there were as many theories as there were participants. Time was fleeting, and we all watched with anticipation each time we went by to see that the sign was still up and in place. I'm still sorry we didn't have a rally complete with the kids' pep band the day the sign appeared, as it was a success! Had we outfoxed LaCoste? Whoopee!

The sign seemed to be high enough that this would be one that would not be torn down. We underestimated the "Night Crawlers," as we had dubbed the sneaky people who ripped down our signs nightly throughout the district. According to reports, a boy was sent up in the dark of night to pull those signs down from the water tower. However, that water tower was just too tall and scary and the kid supposedly froze part way up and had to be helped down. Anyone who has tried to climb a small town water tower on graduation night will sympathize with that anonymous boy. I'm still furious with the stupidity of anyone allowing or encouraging someone to try a stunt like that. Why didn't they just go find their own water tower?! Ha ha. Realizing how high emotions run in the heat of campaigning, we later had a professional sign painter paint the signs up there to avoid the chance of tragedy.

Ag people came through with flying colors! They were not fooled for long by the lawyer farmer but, rather, an inspiration to us when they gave us financial backing. These were not the usual big contributors to political campaigns that were stepping up. Part of Clare's campaign theme was the need of people in agriculture to back one of their own just as the labor unions backed candidates that were oriented their way. One of the frustrations of this goal was the policy of most agricultural organizations, such as the Farm Bureau, that prohibited endorsement of parties or candidates. So we would have to do it the hard way — one at a time.

Our neighbor and great longtime friend, Jim Chipponeri, spent many, many hours delivering hay to dairymen, along with signs for Berryhill and pep talks for his candidate. Dairying is an industry with predominantly Democratic registrations, but he did a whale of a job convincing these farm families that Berryhill was the right man for the job. Were we being too optimistic? I guess none of those democrats could cast a vote for Clare in the primary. We were shooting for the final election.

Our first campaign headquarters was the most rundown, shabby, dilapidated building around! However, it was big, and in our price range — donated! It was a challenge for a housewife to fix up, and I soon had some super help.

Grace Alberta Ray and her three youngsters, Susan, Pete and Paul, showed up with mop buckets, disinfectant, a lot of burlap to hide the ugly, and a lot of creative enthusiasm. We made a huge burlap covered bulletin board where we could post snapshots and copies of the latest news of the campaign, and trimmed it out with felt poppies and greenery. Not too bad I have to say! Those who finished the Taj Mahal had no greater satisfaction than we did at the end of two days of work ... OR grubbier knees!

What money we had was spent on basic organization, buying precinct lists, and operating headquarters. We had two phones and one paid secretary, a dear old buddy of mine, Bev Tillema. She sized up the situation, then wagered a double or nothing salary to be paid upon Clare's victory. Clare couldn't argue her out of it — she fought too hard! As a matter of fact, it seemed that most of our friends had interested parents and children who also wanted to get involved, and they worked long and hard hours right alongside us. Friends offered up dedication and loyalty that no amount of money could have bought. They distributed mimeographed newsletters door-to-door and at shopping centers; addressed and stamped mailers when the budget allowed such luxuries; and when it was all over, they could say with a great deal of satisfaction, "I was involved."

Chapter 4: Supporters Are Golden

Our own kids were super. There is nothing like a common cause to get a family in high gear. With Gaby, our personal challenge to show what could be done in the good ol' U.S.A., she and the kids enlisted the help of all of their buddies.

I have one snapshot I really cherish. It is a picture of Tom and several of his friends, who formed a Berryhill Booster Band. The band played out in front of headquarters one day in the worst looking cut-offs, dumb hats and disreputable hair that you can only imagine — but they made a hit! Music has always been a central part of my life and I began to get an idea around how our kids and their friends could literally play a large part in the campaign, and have fun, too. They were all in the high school band, were good musicians, and could increase their education by becoming active in grass roots politics. All we had to do was ask them, turn them loose, and occasionally hold them down!

We really dreaded that first experience of going door-to-door, so we all went together the first time in Manteca. It was raining, and Lynne was handicapped by crutches from a sprained ankle. No member of our family was more shy at that time than she, but she wasn't about to be left out! Besides, the ankle was rather a badge of honor. The day before we had been at a coffee-klatch at Marie Roen's ranch home, nestled in the eastern foothill area of Stanislaus County. Her home sat high on a hill overlooking the reservoir, nestled in waving grain fields, spring green, and a clear view of the Sierras. It was an irresistible hiking area and the youngsters took off, but were back shortly when Lynne lost the argument with a gopher hole. Casualty #1.

Clare and I attended every public function that we could,

drank an unbelievable amount of coffee at over 100 coffee-klatches, candidate forums, and then we would collapse for five or six hours every night, whether we needed it or not!

Our supporters were getting very nervous as the primary election drew near because our Republican opponents seemed to be spending a lot more money than we were, particularly Ray Simon. Ray had a lot of billboards and an equal amount of confidence in the outcome. We had not run a single billboard outside of the water tower in Manteca OR any ads because our budget did not allow it. Clare was adamant in staying within the budget! Homer Vilas, Rae Codoni, Bev Tillema, Edwina Ground and I, among others, had a number of great ideas for ads, but nothing but cold hard cash could make any of our dreams come true. Still, we were garnering supporters, far and near.

Young Lou Barnett arrived out of the blue, an extremely thin, hungry-looking, bright young man. He seemed to be happier working in politics than putting his feet under the table three times a day. His family was wealthy, but this boy fit in with the whole crew as if we'd known him all of our lives. Lou had an absolutely fiendish sense of humor and thought up many campaign approaches that were wildly imaginative and totally unacceptable! He was a member of the Young Republicans in the state, and he could muster a dedicated cadre of followers from Holy Names College in Oakland who would spend each weekend going door-to-door on behalf of Clare. Lou eventually married Janie, the ringleader of those college girls, creating at least one of several happy endings to romance that bloomed over a precinct list. Without a doubt, there will be a Barnett or two in politics in the next generation, and when there is a Barnett in the White House as President, we intend to have a seat at his inauguration!

Dedicated women from various parts of Northern California quietly assessed the qualifications of the three candidates for Jack Veneman's Assembly seat, and we will never get over our surprise and pride in having these grand gals and an occasional husband join the Berryhilll Bandwagon. They had resented the Republican party's role in trying to hand-pick a candidate and decided to do something about it. Lucky for us! They taught us a lot about walking precincts and putting Ma Bell to good use. When it came to dedication, integrity, and good manners, they won first prize, hands down.

We still were short of cash to run even one ad in the *Modesto Bee*, and the thirteen daily district newspapers. The weekly newspapers were all endorsing Clare's candidacy in spite of the fact that we didn't have enough of the folding green to support them in return.

Our copy was ready to go and we were down to the wire with only one day remaining until the last farm edition of the paper would be out. We were totally frustrated with our seeming lack of funds. The farm folk rallied again, and with a wild hurrah, the ads were rushed to the papers.

We each took off in different directions with ads and cash in hand ... except for yours truly, who got all of the way to Manteca before discovering that I had forgotten the money; I had to go all of the way back to Modesto and get it! Candidates are not considered good financial risks by the people that own papers. No money, no ads. We did finally have a few good billboards in good spots, the best of which was stationed at the busiest intersection in Modesto. Max Hanney had it rented and used his Irish charm in getting the owner to loan it to us. Maybe the underdog image still has a lot going for it, but we had to believe that the last minute one-and-only newspaper advertisement did a good deal to help Clare. It was an endorsement list of hundreds of people indicating the depth of Clare's support throughout the district. We were very proud of that list!

As we assessed the campaign, we were pleased with the response to our bright green and yellow Berryhill signs. The signs had been placed only on private properties throughout the district, where permissions had been given by the owners who seriously guarded them. In the bright spring green of fields and vineyards, which in the months of campaigning had turned from the dull gray of winter, those signs evoked a sense of freshness in politics as well as the sense that the usual hackneyed political advertisement had long lost.

Clare had not made one single political promise to anyone other than to offer himself to serve the people full time, to keep an open door, and a firm promise to be a voice for agriculture in a state where agriculture is the number one industry. He had pledged himself to stay within the budget and had done just that!

Chapter 5: I Did It My Way

For the first time in our married life we would not be actively running a Victory Squad headquarters. Able gals who had assisted me over the years would be in charge of the headquarters that was, as usual, being set up in our dehydrator. Clare and I were somewhere in the limbo of it all. Mildred Vine capably led that set up effort. Homer, Al Pirrone and Joe Geer picked Clare up and carted him off to the golf course to get his mind off the day. It was a cinch that he had done all that a candidate could do, and this would be a good way to pass this day. Meanwhile, I puttered in my garden, talked to family and friends, and relaxed, knowing we had all done our best.

Homer and Carol Vilas had invited all of the regular workers over to their house for dinner and to follow the election returns. We heard that Simon and a number of his Sacramento supporters were joining his staff party at a downtown Modesto restaurant. Pete planned his own party, and we really didn't care where Ernie & Company were going to be. All we wanted was a chance to visit with all of those super supporters and to celebrate. The kids were so excited that it brought tears to our eyes to observe that great confidence. Even Gaby had filed away her doubts and was as crazy as the rest of us! I looked at the shambles of my home that I hadn't touched for a month, and prayed a *thank you* for dear Marge, who not only came in weekly to clean, but was a one woman campaign committee. She struck areas that neither Ray nor Pete would have dreamed of, believe me! She worried about all of us and sneaked in a few extra hours here and there since it was obvious that we weren't going to survive the clutter if she didn't. She could be a rough customer, but was such a loyal and wonderful friend that I only regret that she passed away before the story ended.

Before we left for Vilas' house, my eye was caught by the calendar. All of these busy days filled in with writing. Today, April 22, said very simply *"Don't forget to vote,"* and the future was blank. A strange feeling swept over me after the pace we had been keeping. Well, we had voted and I was sure that the Berryhill Boosters would see that all of our backers did, too. I took a moment in the peace of our home to let God know that I appreciated my life.

The eight of us dressed up and headed out to Homer and Carol's. The Vilas home, which is one of the warmest and most gracious of ranch homes, was ready for a party! They had put up a buffet dinner and a bar and tubs of cold soft drinks. There were about 50 people already there, and as we counted noses it occurred to me that these were people who had never been involved in a campaign before, and were they ever excited!

The kids' band was blasting away on the patio, and it was an optimistic sound for the hundred or so of supporters who began to drift in. Homer had radios connected all over the house and television tuned in as the polls closed and returns began to trickle in from Modesto.

At first, Ray was leading. Clare was showing greater strength than we had expected, however, so we were encouraged. Pete Johansen carried his hometown of Turlock, a strong Republican town, with Clare right behind him. Then the rural precincts began to come in and Homer jumped up on a chair, led a resounding three cheers for Clare, and popped the cork. The first of several bottles of champagne came alive. As our farm friends votes kept adding up, tears were mixed with laughter as we heard the results from Newman, Empire, Salida, Mountain View, and our hometown, Ceres. Clare had 22% of the vote and won the primary. Clare did it his way, and we had proved to Gaby and people from out of the district that grassroots were alive and growing in the 30th Assembly district! God bless 'em.

Then the fun really began! The Assemblymen and State Central Committee people had all gathered in Modesto with Ray Simon, along with various television camera crews and radio announcers. No one but *us chickens* had gathered at the Vilas home. The phone started ringing and they all wanted to know, "*Where the hell does Vilas live and how do we get there???*"

An hour later they started pulling in and confusion reigned supreme. Again, it was a marvelous lesson for our Gaby, as she saw Simon's supporters appear to congratulate the winner, even as they cried tears of disappointment and pure exhaustion. This was also something that she had never seen in Germany, where the party strictly runs the candidates. In fact, it was a first for all of us!

Total votes showed Clare carrying Stanislaus County with 9,537 votes, and the southern part of San Joaquin County that was included in the district with 1,159. The total of the republican vote was 26,032, compared to the Democratic total for three candidates of 21,189.

Lou Barnett, whom Codoni had officially conferred the title of Campaign Coordinator, summed it up pretty well when he was quoted in the Modesto Bee the next day:

"Berryhill conducted a talking, door-to-door campaign. We went to openings, invitations, wherever they occurred, in the city or in the county. I think he won because of this personal contact and the enthusiasm of his campaign workers."

We enthused 'til the wee hours, returned home, wearily falling into bed. We awoke to the surge of happiness in that Clare had won. As Sinatra's song said: *I Did it My Way.*

Chapter 6: Post Primary

In spite of the past thirty days, the campaign began in earnest. We moved to bigger quarters and hired a janitorial service — a much appreciated luxury! It seemed that we had State Central Committee people coming out our ears!

Bev Tillema was ready to put quite a few of the committee people in "File 13", the chuck it bucket) but Clare stepped in and calmed everyone down. He made it perfectly clear that *he* intended to run the campaign, not outsiders, and that our volunteers were to be treated courteously, and that their opinions were always to be seriously considered.

One lesson we had learned about campaigning, was the fact that the candidate is totally dependent upon volunteers. They are there because they believe in you and what you are doing, but they are not employees who can be ordered around. Once you have convinced those people of your worth, then there may be times when the candidate can show impatience or even anger, but not when you are trying to convince people to work for you. Clare took this opportunity to remind all of us who were feeling proud of what we had accomplished without the press, and that this was too big a job for us to handle alone.

The balance of power in the Assembly hinged on this race. The result would mean either Jess Unruh as Speaker, or the Republicans' Bob Monagan would end up in charge. It would make the difference of whether Governor Reagan's programs could get through the legislature or not. We could not afford to let petty differences among staff get in the way of the one overriding goal, which was to win the election. This promised to be a very expensive campaign, with both parties contributing heavily to support television advertising, radio spots, newspaper ads and mailers. Staff would also be paid! We felt like we had already gone from rags to riches.

Clare still had to hold us down occasionally, as we thought that some of the bright young men might have actually been born with telephones growing on their ears. We grew very fond of some of these boys who had never worked in a rural area before and had a lot to learn. We enjoyed letting them discover how farm folks operated.

Two new volunteers from Modesto joined the campaign at this time. One was Dottie Spellman, who had worked for Ray Simon in the primary. She and her husband had lived in Illinois, where the party picked the candidate and, therefore, she had volunteered at the party candidate's headquarters. Dottie had done extensive precinct work in a state where Everett Dirksen, a U.S. Senator, had the volunteers in the practice of doing their homework all of the time, not just at election time, as we seemed to operate. She figured that this guy who had "upset the applecart" must be some special fella! Her warm and bubbly personality was most welcome.

The other new gal was Patty Hollingsworth, who was at that time working on her Masters degree at Stanislaus State College in Turlock. She became so involved that she dropped out of school to devote full-time to the campaign. She had grown up in Modesto, and was a very popular girl with the most beautiful face and a brilliant smile that lit up the corners of the room. Patty had a great sense of humor and had fun writing the *Berryhill Reporter*, which was mailed to all supporters to keep them informed of our progress.

Our slogan (Homer Vilas' invention) *"The Man ... For All Reasons"* was well received. Our messages to the public supporting *"The fighting farmer from Ceres"* and *"Why not a full time farmer for a full time Assemblyman"* also went over well.

The main issues on the public's mind that year involved

campus unrest; a voice for agriculture opposing Cesar Chavez; law enforcement; control of soaring taxes; and school financing. Patty handled her job excellently, and we had a good laugh over our first impression of her. (Curiosity would be more like it!) None of us knew Patty and when she just appeared and went to work at the phone or typewriter, we had a few qualms that she was a spy for the opposition!

Our main committees were formed and they went to work. Wes Sawyer, a member of the State Board of Agriculture appointed by Governor Reagan and a well-known, well-liked local dairyman, was a member of the steering committee. His enthusiasm kept the troops stirred up and moving in the right direction. Henry Veneman, Jack's cousin, served, and without a doubt his even-tempered personality and daily visits to headquarters left a positive attitude among us.

Jack Wherry, who had been active in Johansen's primary fight, gladly switched allegiance to Clare since we were old friends. Jack had signed up to work for Pete before Clare filed. Betty Swann, who always helped Harry Sham on the financial end of his political involvements was new to our side, as was the "Silver Fox" himself. It looked like we had most of the good workers and would have a lot of fun!

We kept emphasizing the need for farm representation in Sacramento, and the present overwhelming number of lawyers serving as legislators. We hoped that Ernie's *"Elect a Farmer"* would come back to haunt him, which I'm sure it did!

A letter of support signed by Governor Reagan, former Lieutenant Governor Robert Finch, and former Assemblyman John Veneman, was sent to voters in San Joaquin County from Assemblyman Bob Monagan, as well as voters in Stanislaus County. John Burton, of Stanislaus county, put out a press release stating that more than $1,000 had been raised by his committee, Democrats for Berryhill. Dick Davey was busy lining up more support from the Democrats as well.

Clare and I were kept on the go, attending coffee klatches. I gained ten pounds eating all of the delicious goodies, while Clare talked — and lost weight! *"Leaner and Meaner"* became his nickname. Due to his varied background, he had friends in every walk of life,

and virtually no enemies. After all, he had operated a trucking business with Jim Kissler when they were still in high school.

After a stint in the service, he had run his dehydrator, first as partner with his dad Claude, and then after he bought the business. He had briefly managed the Boysenberry Association, had served on the school board for nine years, he had Lions Club contacts throughout the district where he had served as a local club president, along with several other social and philanthropic organizations. When you live in an area for so long, you are surprised over the extent of your acquaintances. Everyone liked Clare, and one of the most frustrating statements I ever heard from a potential voter was, "I know both of you guys, Berryhill, and you're too honest to be a politician ... so I'm voting for LaCoste." I ask you!

There were lots of fighting farmers involved in the campaign, with some reaching nearly violent dimensions over the stealing of signs from our supporters' properties. Jim Chipponeri nearly lost his mind trying to supply the signs when they were being torn down or destroyed nightly by the anonymous group that we called the *"Night Crawlers."* Here are several cases, but there were few sign owners who weren't hit. All this did was strengthen Clare's supporters resolve, but these marauders were ingenious, but property owners were more so!

After several thefts of a large sign, Veto Pantaleo got a lift truck and put a sign sixteen feet up in his peach orchard, where it remained intact for years.

Earl Caswell got so mad that he took a large sheet of metal and with a torch, cut a replica of the regular signs, and that thwarted the enemy.

Bob Curci, one of our nearest neighbors, had an ideal corner location on a busy country corner, where the signs could be seen from different directions. He built a sturdy frame, put two large signs up, and the fun began. Bob's wife, Shirley, was also effective in the campaign, having worked in the primary as a volunteer and was now coordinator for the campaign in the Turlock Headquarters. Neither of them had ever been so intensely involved in politics before, but they were really 'gun-ho' over Clare's! The 'Night Crawlers' would take a hatchet to his signs every few nights. He woke up one night, hearing a car stop at his corner, became suspicious and rushed out to catch them – carrying his shotgun, with Shirley, all the while yelling at him that he was wearing only his underwear! He hesitated, and the occupants of the car, possibly seeing this strange apparition, sped away. Bobby Curci has one of the most even dispositions and sweetest smiles on earth, but he had reached the limit of his patience. In addition to being a peach grower, he was also a carpenter. With fiendish glee, he dug a trench in front of his signs, placed a board with finishing nails pointing up, placed the boards in the trench, covered them lightly with dirt and hammered finishing nails from the back of the sign all around the edge. He was insuring that anyone who grabbed the signs would surely be sorry! His signs remained intact for the remainder of the campaign.

Sid Long, another peach grower, actually caught two men one night, recognized them from a local union, and his signs were never bothered again. Sid has one hot temper, and we were glad he had no more incidents!

Many LaCoste signs were torn down, too, but there was one big difference. Apparently the same "Night Crawlers" that pulled our signs down also, indiscriminately and without permission, tacked LaCoste signs all over properties without asking if it was okay to do so. There were many irate property owners who pulled our opponents' signs down from their private property.

We heard another rumor that was impossible for us to verify at the time but seemed logical when we read the list of campaign expenses after the election. The rumor was that brochures were being printed in the basement of the Cannery Workers' Union, with children working there at night. Whether the workers were children was never ascertained, but the head of the union was later fired. One of the complaints against him concerned the printing of a candidate's literature that year, in the basement, which was strictly against the rules. This was the more despicable coming from a candidate who tried to be "*Holier than thou*" and accused us of being the "*big spenders.*" The cost was exorbitant, true, but at least we were honest.

During the primary, we were aware that the State Central Committee had taken a poll throughout the district to find out the name identification of the various candidates. We had never seen the poll, but had been surprised to hear that Simon had the best known name among the republicans. The fact was, as we found out after the primary, Clare's was better known, although not nearly as identified among the public as LaCoste's was. After all, Berryhill's opponent had, a short time before, been shot very seriously. He was attending church at the time, and in a terribly dramatic manner, the ex-husband of one of Ernie's clients, entered the church and at close range shot and injured him very seriously. He had one kidney destroyed and nearly died. There had been much in the papers about the attempt on his life, which naturally gave him very great name identification, albeit the hard way. A few faces should have been red over the results of that poll, but we were too busy to worry about it at the time.

There are more Republicans that vote absentee, historically, than Democrats. Assemblyman Bob Burke, from Southern California, had sent out absentee ballot applications in his own brochures, and we decided to do the same. These applications were then mailed back to our office, and Edwina Ground delivered them personally to the County Elections Department each day. The response was great and we were elated. Many elderly or shut-in people could vote more easily this way, and saved themselves the confusion and possible difficulty of operating the automatic voting machines. This seemed like it would do us each a favor. Additionally, Dr. Grant Bare personally visited all of the hospitals and rest homes to give out absentee ballots.

The two opponents debated on radio station KBEE, on questions chosen by the station, and the frustration of hearing LaCoste become a "*me too*" candidate became apparent. He probably figured that the odds were in his favor, anyway, with 60% of the voter registration going his way, all he had to do was stay close to Clare on the issues and rake in the votes. We had to count on the voters not being fooled, but it made us uneasy.

We participated in two parades in one day during the campaign, a chore which Clare dreaded. He always remembered how he hated to watch the politicians in the parades when he was a youngster and he figured that people still felt the same way. I agreed, remembering how much I loved the horses and the bands, and stood on one foot and the other as politicians rode by. He still wasn't comfortable being called a politician, anyway, so we entered them with little enthusiasm. The boys in the pep band agreed to give us a hand, and we got a wagon of hay, decorated with signs that said "*Smile. This is Berryhill Country!*" The girls had tiny boxes of raisins to distribute to the parade crowds, so we were off to two parades in one day — no mean fete.

The indefatigable Jim Chipponeri agreed to drive a hay truck for us, and his three cute daughters, Cindy, Jennifer, and Matia, helped our daughters hand out raisins and literature along the route. They were a roaring success, as was the band! After the parade that was put on by the farmers in the town of Hughson, we loaded instruments into a pick up and rushed to Oakdale to participate in the annual Rodeo Parade. Very hectic!

The annual 4-H Fair was held a short time before the election, and my neighbor and buddy Bev Zaumeyer and I gathered our 4-H'ers and their sheep in my station wagon and headed for the fairgrounds. Somehow, Clare is always busy at that time of the year, with the previous year finding him in the Orient on a raisin promotion trip, and now this year he had a television crew following him on the campaign trail. He assured me they would get to the fair, which they did, for some good pictures. They then traveled to other appointments, as much ground had to be covered as was possible, and the cost of filming being what it was.

When the day was over, Bev and I discovered that again this year we had forgotten our pitchfork to clean out the stalls. You may not leave the fairgrounds until your stalls have been given permission slips. We looked at those white uniforms of our brood, looked at each other, sighed, and started scooping *"unga-unga"* into gunny sacks. Finished, finally, and extremely grubby, we loaded kids and animals and headed back towards home.

While the kids took care of their animals, we sat down with a cold drink, feet up on the coffee table, relaxed and in a fit of giggles (due partly to fatigue) hashed over what had been a hectic but fun day when Bev suddenly got a look of pure panic on her face.

"Here come the TV people with Clare!" she exclaimed.

"Lock the door," I muttered! There would be no TV for me today. With a frantic look still on her face, she shoved me in the direction of a shower, and in world record time had *"straightened up"* my living room. (To tell you the truth, I was still finding things that she had tucked away a good year later!) I really appreciated her help, but unfortunately the TV people only wanted outside shots and never saw my living room. That's life!

Election Day was drawing near and the pace kept getting faster and faster. One day when nothing seemed to be going right at headquarters, and everyone was at loggerheads, Stevie Recca walked in with sort of a black eye. Little Stevie was in the same Catholic elementary school as Ernie's son. As a member of a minority of Berryhill boosters in that school, Stevie had experienced a number of unhappy experiences. He had Berryhill stickers on his binder, and LaCoste supporters in the classroom would rip them off. He went through quite a few stickers before this particular day, when he had had enough! Although he was smaller than Ernie's son as well as younger, they got into a fight and Stevie had only a moral victory and a beautiful *"shiner"* to attest to his loyalty … along with a new binder. He was one of our exceptional little friends, who, on his own, went door-to-door in his neighborhood distributing Berryhill literature. He made quite a great impression on the neighbors — and on us.

We remember another highlight that happened a few days before the election. Bob Monogan and Dick Lyng, a local boy who had made good as an Undersecretary of Agriculture in the first Nixon administration, were special guests at a packed banquet room of 480 Berryhill Boosters for a *"Salute to Berryhill"* dinner. This fundraiser found everyone in an elated mood. Betty and Bob Stonum had done a beautiful job decorating, and Bette Belle Smith — always there when you needed her — led songs with special lyrics she had written. With enthusiasm, the room sang, to the old [George M. Cohan] tune "Harrigan":

B - E - double R - Y - H - I - double L spells

Berryhill (Berryhill)

He's the candidate we are

Electin' (electin')

All our energies we are

Directin', elect him,

B - E - double R - Y - H - I - double L, you see

He's a guy with a plan

To become our Assemblyman

Berryhill … For me!

Corny it is true, but fun, and an evening all enjoyed. Tom's pep band played before dinner, but due to the fact that we were oversold five days before the dinner, the boys had to settle for a pizza supper elsewhere. We sat at the table absolutely in awe of all that had been done to bring everyone to this point in such a short time. Many of Ray Simon's supporters were there as were Pete's, and they had graciously and, in most instances enthusiastically, thrown their support to Clare after the primary. We were especially pleased to see Nita Veneman, although Jack was still in Washington. It seemed to prove that contrary to the doomsayers, the primary battle hadn't been divisive, it had been informative, fair, and brought diverse groups of people together to elect Clare.

We had garnered the endorsement of all thirteen weekly newspapers in the district, led off by the new editor of the *Ceres Courier*, Lee Roddy; his son, Steve, was in the pep band. Mait Pennington had sold the paper to Lee and returned to more remunerative work in the nation's capital. He kept in touch with us frequently, by telephone. He was very antsy not being directly involved, and many and long were Clare and Mait's conversations as Clare assessed the progress we were making. Mait probed, suggested and fumed. The *Modesto Bee* predictably endorsed LaCoste, as it had in the primary. In addition to the *Bee*'s endorsement of Simon for the Republican primary candidate, we were hoping they would again be proven wrong.

Early in the campaign we had decided against distributing matches with campaign advertising. To emphasize a fresh approach and one related to Clare's agricultural background, we got half-ounce packages of raisins and the kids helped stick on tiny Berryhill stickers to the boxes. We distributed 10,000 boxes and they were a big hit. Lickin' and stickin' are a big part of a political campaign.

Chapter 7: Election Has Arrived

The office was frantically preparing for Eletion Day. We had volunteers coming by car, bus and planes from all over the state to help get out the vote for Clare. Individuals paid their own fare to get here and the only volunteers who got financial help were some of the College Young Republicans who couldn't afford the $15.00 tab. We had no idea how many concerned people there were around the state, and until we were there, we had no idea of the organization that it takes to do the job right. Patty Hollingsworth and her *Charmaritas* in the office had the monumental task of lining up volunteer drivers and cars to drive the out-of-town precinct workers to their assigned jobs. Walk-boards and maps were readied, as were door hangers for those who wouldn't be home the first time a worker rang their bell. Lots of pencils were sharpened, and every worker had a box of raisins.

Jack Wherry, Carol Smith, and Joanne Monaco were in charge of preparing the dinner for all the workers at the California Ballroom. We had rented the largest place in town to accommodate all of the people who would be involved that day and besides, the California Ballroom had a very special meaning for the Berryhills.

A few months before we got involved in the primary, one of Betsy's friends, Mary Lorraine Gomes, decided to run for "Queen of Hearts," the annual fundraising affair for the Heart Association. All of the service clubs in Ceres had already committed their money for the year, so Mary was without a necessary sponsor. She had cut fruit at our dehydrator and made a good impression on Clare with her industriousness, so he agreed to sponsor her. A sponsor agrees to guarantee that the candidates' expenses will be paid, and Mary had already made plans to hold a fundraising dance at the California Ballroom where the Portuguese Pentecost Society meets, and her dad served as President. She had the dinner, band, hall, and tickets, so all we really did was provide moral support and the legalities. We had a wonderful evening at her affair, dancing the Charmarita, visiting with old and new friends, mainly Mary's parents Vic and Mary.

We also met the lady who did the daily early morning radio broadcast in Portuguese, and gave freely of her time to teach English to the immigrants from Portugal. She was a very inspirational lady named Mimi Toste, who really gave me a funny sensation when she kept gently urging Clare that, with his honesty and sincerity, he should run for public office. We laughed and shook our heads. Later, Mimi did some advertising for us in the campaign and was never anything but a perfectly delightful lady, and, we thought, a shrewd politician.

After embarking on the campaign, we were the Gomes' guests at many such evenings, and also attended several parades and traditional Azorean dinners called Sopas with the Portuguese while Mary served as Queen that year. So, there was no other meeting place dearer to us than the California Ballroom for election night!

Rainbow Farms co-owner, Oscar Holt, donated 500 chicken halves for the dinner. When all of the food was ready, Jack Wherry, replete with a chef's hat wilting from working over a hot fire in the kitchen, waited on the group.

About two o'clock in the afternoon I turned on the local radio station and thought I was hearing live coverage of some kind of riot. It was at the Modesto airport and the charter planes were arriving with the volunteers to help on the Victory Squad. There was yelling, shouting and absolute bedlam coming over the airwaves. Patty Hollingsworth was at the airport with her well-planned line-up of cars and drivers to transport the workers. So was Democrat Assemblyman Ken Cory with his troops.

There was an organized demonstration by the Democrats to get publicity, I suppose, and intimidate the people who were arriving.

Later, as the story was pieced together, a motley band of pickets were surrounding the airport with derogatory picket signs and a lot of crude shouting. Patty said that she was so angry she stormed up to Ken Cory, her brown eyes flashing, and they exchanged a few words. It must have looked a bit funny, with Patty barely over five feet high, and Ken a long drink of water!

She said she made him so mad she was alarmed that he might pick her up by her "pussycat" bow and dangle her from the top edge of the mesh fence surrounding the airport! There was no way that airport manager Harry, the "Silver Fox," was going to let that crummy bunch into his airport. So, in spite of the picket, and in spite of the derogatory remark made by LaCoste later, to the effect that he should have brought his Basque sheepherders and their flocks and turned them out on the runway so the planes couldn't land, land they did! The workers poured out, eager for the job at hand. Since I was not present, I'll quote part of the May 22nd issue of the *Modesto Bee*, as it carried the story:

"... a sound truck bearing large campaign signs for the Democrat candidate in the Assembly race, Ernest LaCoste, began taunting the Republicans with 'Welcome to Stanislaus County. This is our election, where is yours? Here they come, you can tell them by the yellow streak down their backs,' the operator of the sound truck, who refused to identify himself, charged. About 70 persons carried a variety of signs which read 'Carpetbaggers need not apply. This is our election, not yours. Are you locusts looking for a plague?' and other slogans."

"Cannery Workers Union Secretary Treasurer, Ted Gonsalves, identified himself to Lt. House as the leader of the group of Democrats. He asked for permission to enter the airport grounds and mingle with about 150 local Republicans who were waiting in cars to drive the workers to the precincts. Gonsalves was told to ask permission from airport manager, Harry Sham, but the union leader was unable to find him. Gonsalves said his group was part of the Democrats for LaCoste organization. LaCoste campaign chairman John Martin denied that the group was associated directly with the LaCoste campaign committee."

There was much more to the article, but this pretty much covers the gist of it, except for a bit of humor that inserted itself into the situation. As the article states:

"While the two party factions glared at each other from opposite sides of a small wire fence, the Rev. Kirby J. Hensley arrived at the airport on his way to a Los Angeles television interview, and began to ordain as many persons as would accept his ministerial certificates. All of the 15 area newsmen covering the arrival of the Republicans left the airport as certificated members of the clergy of the Universal Life Church." Later, rumor had it that several jet planes brought our workers into town, but reading the story in *The Bee*, it says "Two chartered 737 Boeing jets and a D.C. 6 prop chartered flight carried the Republican precinct workers to Modesto..."

It went on to say "The army of Republicans, which also included a small plane load of Ukiah workers and two busloads of volunteers from other parts of the state, packed the California Ballroom during the evening..."

The marvelous thing about these dedicated workers was the stories they told later to prove how every vote counts. Eleanor Ring, then National Committee Chairwoman, related one story to me in confidence about one of her calls in Ceres, but, you ask her!

I will share with you Jean Reinecke's experience: Jean had been hospitalized, with her arm in a cast, when one of the Republican legislators' wives visited her and told her she simply had to get out of there and help on the Special Election the very next day! That's all that redhead needed, and she rounded up some carfuls of helpers from the ranks in Sacramento, and was there, awkward cast jutting up in the air, really quite jaunty! Late in the afternoon, hot, tired and grubby from trudging precincts, Jean and another gal were walking along the roadside when a big truck pulled up and the two fellows in the cab gave long, appreciate wolf whistles. Never one to miss a beat, Jean asked them if they had voted yet. They bantered back and forth until finally, with redheaded impatience, Jean said "Look, we have a lot to do yet. I'm telling you it's really important for you to get out and vote for Clare Berryhill! He's the guy that will understand your problems. I'm Lieutenant Governor Ed Reinecke's wife, and my friends and I thought it was important enough to come down and help on this election, and the least you can do is go vote." Sensing that this was the time to back off from the fiery redhead, they both quickly agreed to go vote right away. As they drove away, Jean heard one of them say, wonderingly, "That crazy redheaded broad really expects us to believe that she's Ed Reinecke's wife!"

Every person walking, persevering, getting out one more Berryhill vote can rightfully take credit for our victory celebration that night — and they do! We never attended a Republican function anywhere in California that someone didn't come up to us and say, "I'm sure you don't remember me but ...," and then tell us another of these stories. For those who doubt the system and complain about the apathy of the American voters, let me tell you, we know the other side.

As workers were congregating at the California Ballroom, ravenous after all of their walking, we had decided to stay out at the ranch until we had a pretty good idea how the election was going. It was a time for the family to be alone for a little while.

All of the family congregated around the fireplace to have a quick supper, and then nervously sat, reminiscing ... and waiting.

Al Pirrone joined us, since he had offered to drive us to town, so we wouldn't have to take our own car. He is one of our best friends and, for awhile, I'm sure he thought we were slightly balmy to be undertaking this whole thing. He loyally worked for Clare's victory. Old grape growers and wine makers stick together.

We were amused to hear from John Burton, then a Democratic Assemblyman, and now a Congressman, his experiences going door-to-door in Ceres for Ernie LaCoste. In his mod clothes and hair, he must have been rather conspicuous in our little town, to say the least.

He knocked on doors in the neighborhood of the Don Pedro Elementary School, where all of our children had attended, and where Bill was then a big sixth grader. It was a heavily democratic precinct, as is most of Ceres, but John was in for a surprise. People would come to the door and he would urge them to go vote for LaCoste, and they would reply, "Isn't that the one who is running against Bill's dad? Ha, don't think I can vote against Bill's dad."

We were proud when the results were in and Clare carried Ceres heavily, when even Eisenhower had not been able to convince our hard-nosed Democrat neighbors to cross party lines. Every time we thought of Dapper John doing precinct work in our backyard, it struck us funny!

Chapter 8: Landslide Berryhill

Numbers, numbers, numbers! Early results were in Clare's favor as the absentee ballets were counted: 847 for Berryhill, 348 for LaCoste, and two for Muratore, the AIP candidate. The outlying votes started coming in and it looked as though we had it. Clare never gets down, but when the votes showed us slipping over 1,000 votes behind, he said, with a weary grin, "C'mon gang. We'd better get into town and thank all of our friends who have been working their tails off for me."

The rest of us were not so composed, but everyone tried to cheer everyone else up. Clare couldn't find out if the Turlock precincts were in yet, and he hadn't given up by a long shot. We were a quiet bunch as we left the ranch with Al, and the rest of the family, Grandma, aunts and uncles, brothers and cousins, followed. Just as we got even with our neighbors the Vissers' almond orchard, about a mile from home, we heard one or two precincts from Turlock announced, and Ernie's lead dropped to around 500. The kids started yelling and pounding one another while Clare yelled for everyone to keep quiet. Al sped up a bit while we listened for some more good news.

It seemed like a really long eight miles to town. Just as we turned off of the freeway into Modesto, the tide really turned and Clare pulled ahead by about 200 votes. Al stepped on the gas, we spurted up the off ramp, made a U-turn and ended up going the wrong way on a one way street! Good thing for us we had such a cool and collected driver. Billy let out a war whoop and threw a tennis shoe right out the window.

As we walked in the back door by the stage, none of us can even remember walking. It was as though throngs of people transported us right up to the stage, where Homer was acting as master of ceremonies, and keeping a running score of election returns on a blackboard. They were not? After just hearing the Turlock results that we had heard in the car, and the cheers that were building up were nearly bringing the roof down! It was definitely one of these moments that never, never, never seem real. I am still so sorry that some of our close friends, such as Big Mike DeRussi from Escalon, missed the end. He had been so upset over the earlier returns that he left before we got there, and did so miss out on all of the fun!

Sitting on the edge of the stage, not bothering anybody, with legs dangling over the edge, was a worried and disconsolate Jim "Chip" Chipponeri. Did he come to life when the vote reversed! Hugging Clare, he shouted above the tumult, "Don't forget, ol' buddy, all I want to do is shake hands with Governor Reagan." He was jostled aside by the crowd that was getting louder, more joyous. Homer was dancing on air and had just about lost his voice trying to be heard over the bedlam. The pep band was blaring away, in deliriously happy disregard for Homer's problem.

Governor Reagan had never before put in an appearance at a special election, but this was an understandably crucial one for him, so he had flown down and had been waiting in lonely isolation at the airport for two hours, waiting for the final results. Who had won?

Chip wasn't the only one anxious to see the Governor. When he finally walked up those stairs, the crowd went wild! I hugged him and didn't even realize what I'd done until the next day. Flashbulbs were popping left and right and my very favorite picture is one with the Governor on one side, the kids in the middle and their jubilant Dad on the other. Bill's expression brings a lump in the throat to everyone who was there that has seen it. He was so happy that he was barely holding back the tears. A pretty exciting moment in a sixth grader's life. I think that Gaby forgot completely that she was German, anti-Republican, and reserved, as she beamed pride and happiness with tears in her eyes at her American dad. She also got to meet the Governor, whom she truly admired. Actually, her anti-establishment feelings weren't too different from our own when we had started [the campaign] such a short time ago.

And Chip met the Governor — one firm campaign promise kept!

As I came back to earth a bit, a glance around the room brought back a flood of memories in my mind of so many old friends who had worked so hard in spite of their initial misgivings to help Clare. I marveled over the many new friends Clare had won over with his honest, sincere, and ethical values applied to the game of politics. Then I cried. Life was surely going to be different. I wondered what Grandma would have had to say.

Our jubilation, while real enough, was tempered the next day when we realized just how close the vote had been; 48 votes had been the magic number, and LaCoste would not concede without a recount. With so much at stake, I'm sure we would have done the same thing.

Acrimony crept into the proceedings, though, as then Assemblyman George Zenovich hinted at irregularities in the Republican absentee ballots. According to the Friday, May 23,1969 Modesto Bee, Zenovich was quoted saying:

"Zenovich said there may have been discrimination against Democrat voters in the

handling of absentee ballot applications by the Republican headquarters."

The Republicans, like the Democrats, had mailed absentee ballet applications to many voters before the election. Zenovich said the applications sent from the Republican headquarters were to be returned to a post office box rented in the name of the Republican headquarters.

"Some Democrats responded to request an absentee ballot and

did not get one," he said. He said there was a possibility the Republican headquarters forwarded absentee ballot applications from Republicans but not from democrats to the election officials. "I'm not saying that happened," he added. "You never know."

Further in the article, Rae Codoni answered this charge; Edwina was too incoherent with rage to be quoted. In answer, Berryhill campaign manager Rae Codoni said the campaign headquarters mailed absentee ballot forms to all registered Republicans and none to Democrats, and that every returned ballot application was forwarded to the courthouse with the possible exception of one which was received after the deadline.

Later in the article, Modesto Postmaster Dan Taylor was quoted as saying:

"... postal regulations probably required the Republican campaign office to use it's own postal box, or address, for return of the absentee ballot applications." He said business reply postage permits must have mail returned to the payee only.

Zenovich also said, "There is a possibility some persons voted by absentee ballot, and then voted again in the precinct."

"I say there isn't a chance of anybody voting twice," elections supervisor Merv Mattos said. When all was said and done and recriminations came to a halt, one weary LaCoste supporter summed it up well by saying, "We screwed up, we screwed up."

It was a frustrating wait while the recount proceeded, with the eagle-eyed partisans keeping close watch on one another, and tempers were wearing thin. We looked askance at LaCoste's lawyers, a battery of lawyers from Chicago and elsewhere, who gave us a sense of uneasiness. Our minds tended at that time to be suspicious of everything the opponent did, and these "city slickers" certainly did nothing to alleviate our fears. We had to look strange to them as well, with Bette Belle, Homer, Edwina and Rae guarding their winner's best interests. They were not about to let those fellows pull the wool over their eyes.

Finally it was done and Clare, who had one vote disqualified in a Turlock precinct, was declared the winner with a razor thin margin of 47 votes, but later picking up three more votes for a total of 50! Just call him "Landslide Berryhill."

Next to election night, the happiest moment for between 100 and 200 of Clare's friends was June 4th, when he was sworn in as the newly elected Assemblyman from the 30th Assembly District. Clare had gone up a day ahead to take care of details and I had been loaned Jack Veneman's state car to drive the children up on the BIG day. Having a notorious reputation for directions, I had made a 'dry run' the day before so I wouldn't get lost. Gaily singing "B-E double R-Y ..." we headed for the Capitol. My confidence was shattered when I finally realized that the directions for one way L and N streets had been reversed overnight, and we finally got turned around and drove into the parking lot. While the gate machine steadily gave me a buzz that sounded like a Bronx cheer, I searched frantically for the window button. I thought to myself, "What am I doing here? Take me back to the farm!"

Getting the window open I yanked the "tongue" from the awful machine, and we dashed for the Capitol. We tore up and down a confusing maze of halls trying to find Clare's office, and just as we were about to sit down in the hall and cry, a group came around the corner. Alice Visser, Ruth Strange and some other friends from Ceres had been sent to look for us. They rushed us to the Assembly chambers where the ceremony was ready to begin. All I wanted to do was sit back, catch my breath, and enjoy seeing Clare seated. Much to my surprise, Assembly-women Pauline Davis, March Fong Eu and Yvonne Braithwaite were asked to escort me up to the front of the chambers to observe the swearing in firsthand! It was a genuine thrill of a lifetime to see, with very great pride, my husband become an Assemblyman — OUR Assemblyman — and a very special guy!

A rousing cheer went up from the gallery at the conclusion

of the ceremony and, with an Irish grin, Bob Monagan had to admonish the gallery visitors that no outbursts would be allowed!

Clare had invited our top-notch volunteer, Patty Hollingsworth, to come to Sacramento to be his secretary, and as the memorable day came to a close, a radiant Patty was royally escorted behind her desk, we said our goodbyes and headed for home.

Chapter 9: Special....and Then Some

As we relate our experiences, some very reflective, and some bordering on hilarity, our minds and hearts reach out to all of the serious people who joined with us to make victory possible. Even the most serious, dedicated partisans were, on occasion, doing silly and unusual things that they would not ordinarily do. The camp did not fit into any of our ordinary life-styles. Emotions sometimes got in the way of practicality or good taste, and became really basic hard-nosed politics.

It is to Clare's credit that the local people whom he chose to help on his campaign were those who were willing to stick to a high level of ethics. They were people who were highly successful in their individual lives, and who lived with the realization that we shared a way of life and a system of government that will always exist under the threat of a different form of government or, at the least, a far different method of solving problems. These myriad people found a mutual enthusiasm in working for the election of one of their own that was willing to forget his usual way of life for the purpose of contributing his time, talent and integrity to better government. We had no intention of making politics our whole future, but the love and appreciation for the opportunities offered by our state and nation demand that some give of themselves in order to make the system work. The time and place was right for us.

These warm memories of the Special Election of 1969 are written in the hope that many of the friends who participated will enjoy the memories, and undoubtedly be reminded of many anecdotes I have omitted. The point to be made is that the grassroots are alive in California, are special, and then some!

Chapter 10: Serving

The ensuing 16 months that Clare served in the California Legislature were an exciting and rewarding period of change in his life. He put together a staff of competent people who had never worked in the wonderful world of politics at any previous time. They had much to learn, and not much time for learning. An open door had been promised to the constituents, and open it was. And did they ever come! No letter went unanswered, and no stone was left un-turned when problems needed to be solved.

Patty, or "Peppermint Patty" as she was nicknamed by those who dealt with her front desk, had her work cut out for her. There was a serious lack of experience on her part concerning typing, to say nothing of her shorthand. However, her loyalty and dedication to her boss was tops!

There was a brief flurry of irritation and excitement when the Assembly conducted a hearing into possible irregularities concerning our use of absentee ballot applications. Cool and collected Edwina was understandably angry over aspersions cast inferring that she had done something unethical in connection with this phase of the campaign.

Upon hearing the charges, Assemblyman Bob Burke, [who served] on the committee hearing, came to her rescue ... and ours. His usual smiling face was red with indignation as he listened to the testimony, and finally cut their allegations to ribbons as he told them that he had used this technique for many years, and it was not something novel or sneaky. Bob had been a pillar of strength and support during the campaign, but we never appreciated him more than at that moment in time.

Summer sped by with the state problems mounting. The State of California borrowed money to operate while the legislature hassled over the gigantic budget required to function in the manner to which we had all become accustomed. Assembly Speaker Bob Monagan had his Irish up and, determined that the taxpayers were going to get their money's worth, kept the legislators in session well into August — when they were supposed to have the budget solved by June 30th!

Meanwhile, the fall elections were drawing near and Clare had choices to make. Should he remain in the job full-time or play hooky, as some were doing, in order to campaign back in the district? In retrospect, it was a very naive crew, all wrapped up in the job they were doing, and totally unaware that the greater mass of voters neither knew nor cared what their legislator was doing for them. What concerned them more was what he wasn't doing for them — right now.

Clare and crew continued to do the job they were being paid to do, convinced that "actions speak louder than words." Sixteen hours-a-day on the job were stretched and expanded to allow for a few speaking engagements. He worked on a talk to retired teachers, some high school government classes, and service clubs. He was beginning to look drawn, and family life became nil. I spent my time helping set up a headquarters again. The same opponent was walking the precinct again. Since our staff was paid by the State of California, Clare did not allow them to be involved at all in the actual campaign. This is as it ought to be, but immediately eliminates the very people who know the most about issues and their boss' accomplishments.

We didn't have Peppermint Patty in any capacity at this time, as she had opted for a return to college for her delayed Master's degree. She certainly had the potential for a different job future. I missed her happy face, straightforward manner, and her rapport with all of our family. Patty and my cousin Ester, who lived in Sacramento, had been my best friends while we nudged our eldest out of the nest. They were both like big sisters to Betsy, who was living in an apartment with her father while attending American River Junior College. These two gals helped me retain my sanity when the combination of legislator and candidate reached the point where the family role had no place to breath, except as an extension of the candidate. It was such a lonely place for this farmer's wife to live.

We also no longer had the help of Rae Codoni this time. He had married immediately after the first election, and was happily involved with his bride, Mary, who was also coping with an illness that incapacitated her for some time.

We limped along, doing the best that we could. Our neighbor and dear friend Bev Zaumeyer ran the office, her grin and impish sense of humor kept the volunteers licking stamps and surviving writer's cramp for days on end from addressing envelopes. Edwina coped with the scheduling and reception desk. Dottie Spellman again organizing the precincts, and the young men from the State Central Committee, again helping us.

During the summer months while Clare was still in session, we campaigned as hard as we could without the candidate. The annual 4th of July parade was held in the usual scorching hot valley weather. Edwina and George Ground had made arrangements for borrowing our neighbor Emmett Visser's beautiful big, white truck for our band to ride in through the parade. The truck was ready, replete with the green and yellow cloth banner which Larry Spellman had made for us. It said, "JOIN THE BERRYHILL BANDWAGON". We had the boys in the band, and a big bunch of the kids' friends. They had a gallon of ice water, a like amount of lemonade, and lots of ice to keep them from wasting away in the heat. Clare, the girls and I were far ahead in the line-up, riding in an antique car. As soon as we made it through the parade route, the girls made a dash for it, and caught the bandwagon to go through again, handing out boxes of raisins. The liquids were used up before the bandwagon even got rolling, it took so long!

Everyone was beginning to look very wilted from the heat.

They had passed the time trying to make Doug VanPelt laugh. He had had his nose operated on to correct a problem, and was healing under plaster, which had to feel miserable in that heat! How he ever played his saxophone under the circumstances. I'll never know why, but Doug never missed out on anything concerned with the campaign.

The truck finally took off and the boys played their hearts out. A game ensued, as the youngsters on the float threw the small boxes of raisins to children lining the street, and then the children would try to throw them back into the bell of Keith Baltz's horn [what kind? a tuba, maybe?], a game that eventually backfired. Since this game involved a safety issue, the public deemed this to be a hazardous practice. We were instructed to cease and desist, so we did.

During the county fair in early August we found ourselves without any 4-H projects, since campaigning and running back and forth to Sacramento left little time for the usual lamb project or my boys' cooking class. We would have felt very much left out if it hadn't been for Janie's pet lamb, Rosie. She was a twin that Janie had bottle fed with T.L.C., and Rosie had the run of the house and yard "while growing up." Although she wasn't big enough to be a market lamb, she was allowed to be a member of the 4-H baby animal farm. Small children and adults alike all got a kick out of watching Rosie follow Janie around, begging for the baby bottle of milk.

At the close of the fair, when animals sometimes get loose as they are being pushed and pulled to load up for the homeward journey, along came Janie and her Dad, with Rosie briskly trotting along behind and jumping up into the pick-up without any guidance at all.

We did the Hughson-Oakdale parade routine again, with Jim Chipponeri organizing the kids' instruments, hay, and literature. It was a fast ride between parades over 25 miles of country road, and as I followed with the girls and the musical instruments, I just knew that Jim was going to lose a musician or two as he cruised quickly along the road! We didn't even care that we were the last one in line at Oakdale — definitely behind all of the horse entries — as the kids in the band played their hearts out. As we watched people sitting on their front porches, tapping their feet and clapping their hands to the happy Dixieland beat, it was all worth it!

The opposition was putting out vicious ads nightly in the Bee, with catchy headlines like "Where did Berryhill fail?" OUr lawyers went over them with a fine-toothed comb and found them within their legal boundaries, but barely. Talk about frustration!

While Clare stayed in Sacramento doing the job for which he had been elected, his opponent was hot on the campaign trail. The Democrats had learned a few tricks from us and were putting them to good use. In the southern section of Stockton, they were waging a whale of a voter registration drive. There were many strong suspicions of irregularities in the method of some of the registrations, but no one was available to track them down. This area was well over 90% Democratic, but historically had been poor at turning out to vote. Privately, Clare and I knew that if they ever succeeded in getting these voters into the polls, it was all over.

We tried to make inroads into the area — a very difficult task. There were several minority races represented and, in addition to the real problem of widespread poverty, these people were isolated from the larger part of the community by lack of transportation as well as philosophical differences. We met some very fine people who were working against great odds within that neighborhood to provide practical solutions to some tough problems. As far as I know, they are still there, they are still trying, and they still have the same or similar problems.

Bob Monagan finally adjourned the legislative session on August 22nd, and Clare started to campaign, despite being mentally and physically tired. He still devoted half of his time, once back in the district, to constituent problems, rather than out glad-handing the voters and giving speeches. It was not a grand and glorious period with even our most loyal supporters pushing and pulling a visibly weary candidate to make up for lost time. We waged a clean campaign and a solvent one again, with no mud-slinging, in spite of what was flying our way. Clare's record would have to speak for itself.

Chapter 11: Chaos moving into the Election

Waging his own vigorous campaign was an American Independent Party (AIP) candidate, flailing away at the issues of big government, big spending, and law and order, as if he alone could solve these problems. It didn't matter to him that Clare and the Republican administration had passed the strongest law enforcement bills of any California legislature. There was a substantial Bible Belt fundamentalist population in the district, and they seemed to be listening all too attentively to the man who was coming on the strongest. With

Clare's election in 1969, and finally a Republican majority, the Reagan administration had been methodically and successfully tackling those problems. No one felt more strongly about violence on our college campuses than Assemblyman Berryhill. Here is an example:

I accompanied Clare and two other Republican legislators to the Fresno State College campus to speak to the students. The Free Speech Movement at Berkeley had started a pattern for other campuses to follow, and many lawmakers were understandably reluctant to set foot on the California campuses. The free give and take within the classrooms was very refreshing, and I sat back and enjoyed the day. The students had many penetrating questions and did not seem to resent Clare's stand on not lowering the age for voting and drinking, even though they disagreed with him. On the other hand, a wishy-washy "maybe yes, maybe no" answer by one of the other Assemblymen brought out a "typical politician" expression on the faces of the young people. I was proud and pleased with the progress of the morning as we gathered in the beautiful student center, quiet now, where a large gathering of students had assembled.

State Controller Hugh Fluornoy was having a luncheon meeting with the college President, while Clare and Kent Stacy, then Assemblyman from the Bakersfield area, were to answer questions from the students. There did not seem to be any faculty type members in the audience but we didn't think too much about it, as I joined another lady in the party and we relaxed, prepared to enjoy a lively rap session.

Looking over the group it was hard to peg them, but the questions seemed to reflect a liberal viewpoint. They wanted straight answers which Clare was happy to give them. Sprinkled throughout the room were quite a few Mexican-American Educational Opportunity Program (EOP) students, explained a young man sitting next to me. Across the aisle and a bit in front of me, a blonde, balding, crew-cut heavyset older fellow leaped to his feet and, with a shout, threw the first egg at Clare. Bedlam broke loose as a barrage of eggs came flying at him from all over the room. There were shouts of Chicano Power, the making of references to Clare's background as a grape grower, none of which were even slightly complimentary.

Two things I will never forget about those few minutes are my immediate rage at the ringleader and the almost uncontrollable urge to leap on him and bite, kick and scratch, and the opposite feeling of intense pride in Clare's handling of the situation. He was ducking a lot of eggs and not missing a beat in his remarks. The regular students sat, stunned, unable to cope with what was happening.

One egg finally smashed on Clare's jacket, but the rest of them were dripping from the furniture, paneling and lamps in this beautiful new center. As quickly as it started, the ringleader gave the signal to clear out. As they filed out the door still hollering, the man in charge, certainly no Chicano, turned and shook his fist at Clare and yelled "Next time it will be a bullet in your forehead instead of egg."

Clare never left the podium and continued to speak for a half hour, with all of the students indicating outrage at what had happened, and admiration for his conduct. I sat and shook. Clare finally asked Kent Stacy to take over the meeting and it was closed quickly. It seemed incredible that a college would invite politicians onto a campus without having a single faculty member present as he spoke. One thing for sure: they didn't nickname Clare the "Fighting Farmer from Ceres'" for nothing!

Later in the month a formal apology came from the administration of the college. We were more concerned that the leader of the hullabaloo be dealt with in a firm manner so future meetings would avoid having a repetition of the violence. Incredibly, the administration chose to turn the investigation of the situation over to the student body, who, in their infinite wisdom, declared that no real harm had been done. It therefore came as no big surprise to pick up the evening paper a few weeks later and read that radicals had bombed and destroyed the computer center at Fresno State College.

When the AIP candidate was decrying violence on campuses, Clare was a full-fledged veteran of that particular war, and had his record before the voters with co-authorship of many tough bills relating to this very issue. As a result of this group of new laws, the head of the college administrators were greatly strengthened. During the following year, the occasions of violence decreased dramatically.

Many voters don't take the time to read or analyze voting records, however, and we were increasingly concerned over public reaction to the third-party candidate. He was more likely to pull votes away from a Republican candidate than a Democrat, and we couldn't afford too many votes going that direction. Clare had a good voting record, but suffered the fact that the special election had come after the deadline to author bills so he was limited to becoming co-author on the bills he wished to support. Sixteen months was hardly long enough to get your feet wet as a legislator.

We didn't have long to wait to see the results. Election day rolled around again and Clare's supporters were jubilantly confident that he would walk away with the election this time. They were sure the vitriolic mudslinging attacks in the paper would backfire on their authors. Many were only vaguely aware of the massive voter registration drive conducted in Stockton, and they considered the AIP candidate a mere annoyance!

Clare received 10,000 more votes than he had in the special election, but lost the election by 1,200 votes, ironically the same number that the AIP candidate received. In South Stockton, mini-buses which were manned by Democrats from all over the state hauled 80% of its voters to the polls. In the previous election, a mere 15% of these same voters had cast their ballots. In case these voters ran into trouble figuring out how to work the voting machine, a simple white card was handed to them with two names for them to match up and pull the lever for — Jess Unruh for Governor, and Ernest LaCoste for Assemblyman. Strangely enough, rage within me kept any tears from being shed that night or almost at all as far as losing was concerned. We had worked on too many campaigns besides our own not to be able to read the message loud and clear.

With a sigh of relief that it was over we returned back to the ranch pick up the pieces of our life that we had been missing, including old friends, hunting, skiing, and a trip or two. We thanked God that we had such greater good fortune as to have this to come home to with no inclination towards bitterness. At least not much....

Chapter 12: The Aftermath

It seemed that every Berryhill supporter wrote a letter expressing their sorrow. One letter in particular was unforgettable, because it concerned a student. These young people had made the whole election event worthwhile. The fact that so many young people had become involved as volunteers and had worked so conscientiously for Clare, we considered this perhaps his greatest contribution to our ideal of good, clean politics.

This particular young fellow had accompanied Clare to a meeting with Congressman John McFall at the high school in Patterson, a west-side rural community in Stanislaus County. In his letter he indicated how he had been inspired by Clare's honesty and knowledge of the issues, and admired his practical approach to solving problems. It was quite a long letter, and after reading it we finally cried tears of despair and frustration for having such a brief time to make a contribution.

A letter with a funny side arrived about this time. We hadn't heard from our old friends Ted and Helen Sypolt for a long time. Ted was busy at his job as an administrator of the Agriculture Department at College of the Desert, in Palm Desert. Helen had called us the day after the special election to complain that they didn't get any results on Clare's election down in the desert. We assured them that Clare had indeed won that one, even if it was by a hair's breath. They had heard only one radio report and in that period he was trailing. So, a few days after Clare was retired from public office, a very formal letter of congratulations arrived from old buddy Ted. Apparently this time the last word broadcast in Palm Desert was that Berryhill was winning!

We all learned so much of value during 16 months in office. We made so many lasting friendships that we had surprisingly few regrets over putting this period behind us. If Grandma had still been with us I could have reminded her that life had never been dull since I married farmer Berryhill! Exciting, challenging, and rewarding ... but never dull.

Clare survived his first real defeat in life with flying colors. I nurtured a few concerns about his ability to take such a setback since he had never lost a battle before, but as he often said, "Worry nothing." He and the boys enjoyed the greatest duck hunting season of their lives, and the girls and I enjoyed the serenity of what was as close to a life as we had experienced for quite some time.

We indulgently chuckled over some die-hard Berryhill supporters, like Vivian Codiga, who retained a supply of bumper stickers. Every time she got her car washed, she stubbornly replaced the old one with a new one.

Our family and friends were glad to have us home again and life soon regained the old pattern that the stormy sea of politics had briefly disturbed. Life, like the few ripples out in our pond, was smooth.

We watched with interest and growing concern as the new Assemblyman took over our district. As the months went by we saw a buildup of very vindictive behavior towards all of our former supporters and an arrogance that was most disturbing. Taking the brunt of the attack was Wes Sawyer, Clare's former chairman of "Farmers for Berryhill". Wes, in addition to being one awesome man, was known worldwide for his accomplishments as a dairyman and breeder of superior livestock. He and his neighbors along the Tuolumne River in the eastern foothills of the county found themselves the target of an unbelievably vicious campaign by the newly elected Assemblyman.

The Modesto Bee published many stories referring to allegations that the farmers on the river were causing pollution, that they were alleged to have shot at trespassers, and were accused of being 'greedy land barons' keeping the public from access to the river. It was claimed that they kept recreational kayakers from year-round use of this stretch of the water. These allegations had been made during the campaign and Wes and his neighbors, dubbed the "river rats," fought with increasing anger and frustration the unfounded list of charges.

Wes also served on the State Board of Agriculture, and he caught the heat there, as

well. The Assemblyman tried to get him, it would seem, in two ways. First, he introduced a bill that would open up the Tuolumne River along the stretch where the cattle ranchers had their range land along with their fences. Ah yes, the fences that one would think were placed across the river solely to stymie those who wanted to paddle their kayaks down the river. No matter to those interested in recreation that when the water was low the fences were necessary to keep the cattle within the boundaries. They also easily forgot or didn't know that the trickle of water in late summer made it virtually impossible to paddle anything along that particular stretch of the river, which was shallow and ugly!

The impression given through the press was that the "greedy land-barons" must be taught a lesson. Wes and the "river rats" fought like tigers against the vicious and untrue allegations as well as against the Tuolumne River bill in Sacramento. Although he was no longer a legislator Clare still had many friends in the capitol, and he kept in touch. A valid point he made as a conservationist was to point out that the nesting places of the protected species of Blue Heron would be disturbed by public access to this stretch of the river. Another valid point brought out was the fact that even though there was public access to the river downstream, the property owners had granted permission to use that particular area when there was an adequate flow to Boy Scout troops and other responsible individuals.

Eventually, after much senseless rhetoric the author of the bill, our old opponent watered it down, so to speak, until it really accomplished nothing. The bill was finally killed in the Senate Natural Resources Committee, where it was felt that they had much more important "fish to fry."

The second prong of the attack on farmer supporters of Clare's came in the form of a bill to freeze the acreage that could be planted to peaches. For several years the peach growers had very successful years in the largest peach growing area in the world, principally in the Hughson area. The high prices resulted in over-planting and a drastic drop in the return to the grower. Many non-farmers saw this as a way to have a fine tax write-off if they were in a financial position to need this kind of relief. These individuals and corporations who entered the peach farming business were not totally concerned with making a profit and as the market became glutted the legitimate peach grower took a bath. This was another issue that had come up in the campaign with our opponent urging drastic change to "protect" the real farmer, and Clare urged caution, pointing out the fact that he and many grape growers had survived fifteen years of poor financial return but that the trend had changed finally to the grape growers' advantage. The most efficient growers were still in business.

While recognizing the reality of the peach growers' plight he cautioned that acreage limitation was a drastic approach, and alien to the free market system. Peach growers that were going under found little solace in his words, but Clare kept the door open, acknowledging that the understood the seriousness of the problem, and had no "instant answers."

Wes, on the State Board, opposed the peach bill, and although it got through the legislature, it was eventually vetoed by Governor Reagan. Wes took a lot of heat on this issue. Eventually the public tired of the subject, and our lives settled down to the placid pace of the Tuolumne River.

We were enjoying relative prosperity after long years of tough sledding in the wine grape industry, and developing thirty acres of almonds. Clare had learned the inherent dangers of "putting all of his eggs in one basket," and had a small acreage of peaches as well as investing in some real estate. An opportunity presented itself to sell one hundred acres of grapes and we took it, thus getting into the most financially solvent position we had ever had. Contrary to what much of the public believes about "fat cat farmers," most of their wealth is tied up in land and equipment, and it is often only when they sell property that they have anything in the pockets that jingles. So we decided to live a little!

Part two: AND THEN SOME!

Chapter 1: It Begins..Again

In late fall, rumors were wafting down from the Sierras that Steve Teale, our State Senator, was retiring. He had served twenty years and also had small children from a second marriage that needed more of their father's time. His first wife and children were killed in a tragic auto accident.

Friends started approaching Clare to see if he would run and he would say, "No Way!" We blithely went about our own business of enjoying the Christmas holidays with family and friends up at Dr. Den Dulk's cabin at South Lake Tahoe. We gazed appreciatively from the deck at the broad and multi-tones blue of Lake Tahoe, ringed with snow covered peaks and the glitter of neon lights from the gambling strip. To our left, the face of heavenly Valley, a dramatic ski area that was intimidating to behold. Clare and the kids could handle it, although Bill got stranded on the Waterfall run when he made a wrong turn. Fortunately one run later, Clare discovered him and guided him on down. In no time he was coping with anything the big kids tackled. I stayed with the easier slopes and had a ball. We skied, slept like logs, played dominoes, and when it snowed for a couple of days and nights, the mountain turned into an unbelievable fairy-tale beauty. Clare and Bill built model airplanes to pass the time. It was a perfect family vacation. With friends of our gang that dropped in to visit, we ended up with wall-to-wall sleeping bags at night, in addition to four lovely bedrooms.

In February, we went with some new friends to Spain and made plans to go with them to Punta Pescadero, a remote fishing resort in Baja, Mexico. We, who never traveled often or extensively, couldn't seem to go far enough often enough, or fast enough. God bless Clare's Mom and my Aunt Peggy and Uncle Kyle, who enjoyed staying with the kids at home or at their homes.

On the warm, sandy beach in Baja, we spent hours with Sally and Oscar Holt discussing philosophy, religion, favorite books, and idly watching as myriads of infinitely delicate yellow humming birds industriously harvested the sweetness of the many flowering shrubs. How simple and pleasant their lives seemed, as did our own. Some days it seemed that our only obligation for the day would be to go down to the shore, turn over a rock and patiently watch it 'walk away'. All of the many tiny creatures that lived in the rock would head for less exposed places to live. We went fishing and took picnic lunches to beaches where not another soul would be seen all day. The incredible blue of the Sea of Cortez was just as Steinbeck had described it, looking like a huge bottle of bluing had been poured into it. I took water colors down to the beach and came home with some sketches for Sally and Oscar complete with real sand.

During one of our conversations about politics we got into plotting a campaign of ideal proportions for the mountains of Steve Teale's 3rd mountain district. It extended from the southern tip of Stanislaus County to the Oregon border on the eastern edge of northern California. Five hundred miles as the crow flies creates interesting problems for a candidate. Clare mentioned what fun you could have in a motor home, taking the entire family through the small farming communities of the valley, up the old 49er trails of the Mother Lode circling halfway around Lake Tahoe up to the northern cattle and wildlife lands of Modoc and other far north counties. All of us had something to contribute and all of a sudden we realized that we were breaking our self-imposed rule of 'not getting involved again'. We jumped up, hopped into our rented Volkswagen Safari and headed for a wild ride on the curving cliff hugging road to a nearby resort for an evening of fun. We called this dirt road the 'Baja 500', although it was only eight miles long, because Clare and Oscar loved to race the clock to compete with each other on their driving skills. Sally and I dubbed them 'Oscar Oldfield' and 'Barney Berryhill'. More than once the good Lord answered our prayers by placing a bony and lazy milk cow smack in the middle of the road to escort us at a leisurely pace through some of the hairier sections of the road.

We returned from Punta Pescadero tanned, relaxed and vowing to go back as soon as possible. It would be a trip next time with all of the kids to share this wonderful spot. You can rest assured that it didn't happen for quite some time. Once back home, curiosity was aroused by many people because our new Assemblyman was talking about running for the Senate seat being vacated by Teale, thus leaving the assembly seat open once again. Again Clare was saying "Not Me!"

We attended an annual Growers' Harvesting Committee dinner at the Racquet Club in Modesto, happy after all of our traveling, to visit with so many of our old friends in farming. Of course, the Assemblyman was present, but they had not chosen to seat him at the head table, a rather deliberate slight. As the party was getting ready to break up I felt an emotional chill as the Assemblyman approached Clare. , not wanting to have to talk with him, eased back into a cluster of friends. If we all had not heard the conversation I wouldn't have believed it. It went more or less like this:

Assemblyman: "Clare, I'm thinking of running for Teale's seat in the Senate. How about taking over your old seat in the Assembly? can almost guarantee you that no one will run against you."

Clare: Grinning and seeming to be completely relaxed said "Why Ernie, you know me. That just sounds too easy. If no one runs against you I wouldn't let that one pass and give you a free ride."

I felt white hot anger choking me, and then noticed a look of dumbfound amazement flash across LaCoste's face as we all turned and left for home. Clare gave him something to chew over that night. The very next day Ray Simon called Clare to tell him that his old opponent had called him to ask if the republicans had lost their minds. Clare told Ray about the previous evenings' conversation, and also that he was contacting Assemblyman Gene Chappie of the 6th mountain area assembly district to urge him to run. Clare felt he could give him some valuable help in the 'flat-lands'. After he finished talking to Ray, we sat down on the fireplace hearth sipping a cup of coffee, and going over the grotesque unsavory conversation of the night before. Clare was kicking himself for letting his temper do the talking, which is not the way it had seemed to the rest of us. Anger flared again. "Babe" he said, I couldn't let him get away with such a sleazy remark as that." Anguish showed in his face as he turned to me and said I promised you I was going to stay out of politics, and I mean to but,". He hesitated groping for words. "Sometimes it seems that I'm being pulled, pushed, or led in ways I just don't want to go." My heart ached for him, not only for the present situation but this was a deep rooted feeling that my Welshman did not express freely or often. I said we'd just have to pray for guidance remembering, "Not my will but Thine be done." I assured him that whatever he decided would be fine with me, but we had to let go of the problem before an answer would come. When he decided what he wanted, to stick with it, I'd stick with him.

Clare talked with Gene Chappie several times while Gene was trying to decide what he should do, as he had his own political future to consider. Gino is a very popular person in the Mother Lode area he represented, and he was a likely candidate for Congress at some future time. He was sure of his seat as an incumbent and concerned about his opponent having the large population center in Stanislaus County, where Gene was relatively unknown. We waited patiently for some time without hearing from him. Ray Simon was getting anxious too since he had decided that if Clare didn't run for the Assembly, and La-

Coste didn't either he would make a run for it. Clare assured him there was no way that he would run for the Assembly, but if Ernie LaCoste thought he had the Senate seat handed to him on a silver platter, he had another think coming. Still we waited to hear from Gene....and we waited. Just as we were really beginning to wonder what was going on in Sacramento we got a late evening phone call from Chappie. I'm sure both our hearts were pounding like we had run a mile race, for this would have to be the moment of decision. My feelings were so mixed since I knew that if Gene ran for the Senate seat we would be relieved and pleased, but on the other hand we had talked about the campaign so much that it was beginning to seem very real.

"Well Gene, what's the good word?" asked Clare. He remained silent, listening for about five minutes, a grin slowly spreading across his face and finally he doubled over with laughter. was beside myself! Soon it became apparent that the air was very blue at Gene's end of the phone in Cool where he and Paula lived. To put it briefly, our Assemblyman had brought his wife and two children into Gene's office to make a deal with Gene. n his inimitable manner he pointed out how badly his family needed him to get the job and hinted that he would be inclined to back Gene for Congress if he would not run against him in the State Senate race. Our Paisano hit the roof and sent him packing and then had called us from home to urge Clare to file saying that Clare had the support of the Capitol Republicans. Clare didn't have to call Ray Simon to tell him, because Ray got tired of waiting and filed that very day.

Clare and I stood there in the kitchen grinning like a couple of idiots at each other. The kids were crowding around catching the mood since they had wanted their Dad to run all along. Clare and I remembered all too well the strain on family life so had more reservations than they did. We spent the evening calling friends, answering the phone, and making rapid plans. When the evening was over, Clare's concerns about being pulled by forces greater than he, seemed to hang in the air. The principles that led us into politics the first time were still unshakable, and our hope to bring a voice for agriculture and honest politics with a candidate of high ethics and integrity were still right there in Clare Berryhill.

Clare had a long talk with Rae Codoni to ask him to manage the campaign and if we were successful, to become his administrative assistant. Rae went home to talk it over with his wife Mary and bless her heart, she said "GO", although she surely had many reservations.

Edwina Ground and Bev Zaumeyer were ready to go, and Betsy and I started digging out campaign notes, maps etc., that we had hidden during the bonfires that had followed the last election. Clare didn't know we had saved anything but old stationery that was used for scratch paper. There was instant and total commitment on the part of all of our family and friends. In addition to all our more noble concerns, we had a score to settle. The candidates each had one win and this could very well be looked at as a winner takes all situation.

Bright and early the next morning, Clare and I met Edwina and a photographer at Merv Mattos' election department to take out filing papers. Our supporters fanned out to get signatures and that evening we met back at our house to celebrate the start of the campaign. Annalee and Frank Dompe, dear friends and die-hard supporters from Crowslanding, arrived, wearing big grins and lugging a case of champagne. It was a happy evening.

The phone rang at seven the following morning and a man who said his name was Gil Stokes asked to talk with Clare. His voice was very authoritative, so I got Clare and heard him tell the stranger to come on out to the ranch right away. Clare had been invited to appear on a local television station at ten and had only a short time. Clare had a funny look on his face as he came up and off the phone. "I'll be damned" he said. "That guy is filing as a republican candidate for the 3rd Senate seat. He's a commander in the highway patrol and says he's the only one who can beat LaCoste, and that I should withdraw." We got the giggles and were wiping tears from our eyes as Edwina arrived, and as he relayed the fellow's message to her, she couldn't see what was so funny and further more didn't know why Clare should give the guy the time of day. "Wait a minute," Clare said, matter of factually, "Let's see what he has to offer. He may be the candidate we've been looking for all of this time. He is from the mountains and inferred that he had Steve Teale's blessing so let's just listen to him."

We waited, full of curiosity about this gentleman of whom we knew nothing about. After what seemed like eons, Captain Stokes arrived, a man with a decidedly military appearance, steely eyes, firm handshake, and a quick brush off for the two obviously nosy ladies present. In a suave manner, he said he really enjoyed ladies in the right place and at the right time, inferring that this wasn't in either category. So we parked ourselves at the dining room table with several steaming hot cups of coffee and ears practically flapping as we strained to hear the conversation in the living room. Finally we heard Clare get up and say "This has been most interesting, Gil, but I've got to get cleaned up and get to the TV station." Gil followed him down the hall to the bathroom, continuing to present his reasons why Clare should not run, but should support him. My prejudices showing a wee bit, I muttered ungraciously to Edwina, "Are we supposed to stand up and salute?"

He finally left and Clare was almost late for his appointment so he merely said "Well, here we go again. Another contested primary!" Still looking serious he said "He may be tough I just don't know."

As a matter-of-fact, the evening paper listed not two but three republican candidates. n addition to Stokes, looking rather smashing with his highway patrol cap smartly tilted and closely trimmed mustache, there was another total stranger by the name of Bill Steele. Steele was from North San Juan, owned an ice cream parlor, was a retired Marine and he bore a slight resemblance to Archie Bunker of TV fame. Well, we were, indeed, 'still in the family', republican, that is, and we would see what we would see.

The democratic opponent was still in session in Sacramento finishing up the last of his first term in office. He didn't have any primary opposition however and was undoubtedly having a few good laughs at our expense. We didn't have time to worry about him, though, as we all pitched in with enthusiasm to open an office in Ceres, our home town. Bev Zaumeyer was hired to run the office with Rae as chairman. Bev had been antsy because she had a full time job during the previous campaign and had missed out on all of the excitement, which she loved. We leased a motor home to use as a mobile headquarters much as we had discussed with Sally and Oscar in Baja. We dubbed it the 'Big Green Machine' (BGM for short), since it had a special paint job in forest green and yellow, our colors, and script letters on the side that said 'Join the Berryhill Band Wagon – 3rd Senate District'. We had found out that there were 23,000 miles of road in the district and I vowed to get the names of all of the towns painted on the BGM by local people as we visited each town. I mean to tell you we were rolling!

Chapter 2: ...and...We're Rolling!

During the spring primary months, Clare and I would use our car to explore the district. The young people joined us on weekends until school was out and we could stay in the motor home. There was a lot of territory to cover and work to be done, and with a primary contest, no Republican Central Committee or club could either take sides or contribute money to any one candidate. Chappie was also hampered from helping Clare for the same reasons. However, we were all given opportunities to meet the public through many, many 'candidate' nights, where each Republican makes a statement then answers questions from the audience. This is a time when certain local issues are explained, and the candidate has an opportunity to get a better feel of the people in the district. Sometimes the meetings can get pretty hilarious.

The first humorous evening involved the candidates pitch to Stanislaus County Central Committee members. Ironically, we were not present. Clare and Rae's strategy was to get Clare into the mountains to get acquainted and to spend very little time close to home. The only mountain county where Clare was acquainted to any great extent was Tuolumne. Clare's family had built a cabin at Leland Creek, on highway 108, in the depression years of 1933 and 1934, with a lot of help from their friends. We had all spent many happy times in that cabin and knew a few people well enough to muster a nucleus of supporters.

Clare had hiked and fished all of his life in that portion of the high Sierras that surrounded the Sonora Pass. The previous summer had realized a long held dream of our family. Clare got us all on horseback for a pack trip to Huckleberry Lake, 27 miles south of Kennedy Meadows, right at the border of Yosemite National Park. That was some ride, especially for a bunch of greenhorn females, but we enjoyed ten heavenly days without seeing another living soul. As the summer of the campaign progressed, we got out our pictures of that perfect vacation and tried to decide if we weren't more than a little 'crazy'. Actually, Huckleberry was in the 3rd Senate District, but we felt compelled to go where there were doors to knock and people to meet. Heaven would have to wait.

Rae had ranched in Tuolumne County at one time and prevailed upon one of his old neighbors to become Clare's county chairman. The Rosasce family was well known and highly respected cattle ranchers. We were delighted to meet Otis and Jean, and one night they had Clare, Tom, me and Doug Van-Pelt over for dinner. The boys practically drooled as John sliced one of the biggest roasts they had ever seen. We appreciated them more and more for different reasons as the campaign progressed. They were willing to take the time in the effort needed to run the campaign in their county, and what a job they did. The kickoff was an old fashioned whistle stop steam engine train ride from Jamestown to above Sonora and back. I think Clare and I walked a hundred miles on that train, trying to meet everyone and also visit with old friends. The train was decked out with red, white and blue bunting and a large round poster at the very back where Clare delivered a Fighting Farmer' speech at the Sonora depot. There as a catered dinner by Jack Eddy from Twain Hart Lodge. There were a dozen or so volunteer gals all dolled up in red, white and blue dresses, to act as cocktail waitresses. In the club car there was a dance hall costumed gal playing a really mean honky-tonk piano. A young man was playing banjo, and the crowd was happily singing, lurching with the movement of the train, and having a blast. When we arrived in Sonora, much to our surprise, we were enthusiastically greeted by the mounted and uniformed Tuolumne County Sheriff's Posse. Whooping and hollering, they circled the train, lassos waving and occasionally dropping the rope over startled but thrilled passengers. Tom's band met us at the station platform where they played their hearts out to the happy crowd, then they joined us for the remainder of the trip, and had dinner aboard the train.

Tuolumne was off and running a creative and enthusiastic campaign. We were concerned about the local paper whose editor was a pretty strong Democrat, but the first article, written by a young new report, was very complimentary. We hoped that as the editor got to know both candidates he would be neutralized at the least.

While most Republican candidates were still avoiding college campuses, Clare was going whenever invited. Good grief, with five teenagers on good terms with him in our own family, we figured he'd do just fine – and he did. In Columbia, the charmingly restored gold rush town near Sonora, we had an old friend in Dusty Rhodes, President of the local satellite campus of the Yosemite Junior College in Modesto. Jim Oller was attending the school at that time and he was just like one of our own kids. Jim was a hard working young man with a real flair for politics. Another young Republican, Mark Bennett, was raised in the area. Mark served as Clare's youth chairman for the county.

One day we dropped into Jamestown to say "hello" to Lillian Snyder, a very controversial and highly principled woman whom we had met recently. As a judge she could in no way be involved in politics, but she told us one story that let us know where she stood. She got a phone call from Ernie LaCoste asking her to help him. She told him she sure would. She'd help push him right over the ledge, or words to that effect. When the campaign was over, Lillian sent me a beautiful sweater she had knit for me, her way of keeping out of trouble but still letting us know how she felt.

Ruthie Clark of Twain Harte is another special lady from Tuolumne County, a wonderfully vivacious seventy-five year old, who wrote a column for our monthly publication in California, 'The Republican'. She left an indelible picture in my mind's eye from the train trip. Elfin grin on her round little face, blue eyes sparkling and white hair glistening in the sunshine. Ruthie, leaning over the railing on the back of the train, toasting the Sheriff's posse. She was dressed in her 49ers costume, a lovely Chinese kimono, reminiscent of the heritage from the Chinese who did so much to help develop the West. Somehow that kimono did not look the least incongruous on this lady of Scottish descent.

Another character we met was a fellow from out of state who knew about the campaign. He did add a bit of spice to one of the more ordinary days. We were traveling in the motor home with Bev Zaumeyer and our driver, old school chum, Richard Smith. Reaching the community of Valley Springs, we decided to stop for a bite at a little restaurant that Clare had visited before. After a short chat with the owner, we were confronted outside by a fellow in a badly beat up old Cadillac. He was eyeing our gaily painted Big Green machine and seemed to be ogling Bev! "Are you a Berryhill?" he asked. "Sure you are, he answered himself. I've got your brochure right here." He pawed through the papers in the car, which looked strange, with a bed made up in the back seat. Sure enough, he came up with one of Clare's brochures. Grinning he said, "I'm Joe Comferti from Reno, but I get around and meet a lot of people." I was puzzled by the whole affair, but Richard Smith cracked up after we got rolling again, and he had to explain to me that as he had heard, Joe ran a high class whorehouse in Nevada. Help does indeed come from unexpected sources!

Chapter 3 Territory

We had our hands full with the primary fight with both Bill Steele and Gil Stokes. Gil's legal residence was in Calaveras County where Senator Teale lived. However, we discovered that he actually resided with his new bride in Sacramento and maintained a house trailer in the mountains. He had not been considered an actual resident by the local people for about seven years. We were not too concerned about either of them for the basic reason that this was a Republican primary and Clare was a bona fide working member of the party, known to others throughout the state. I, too, had most recently served on the board of the Central Division of the California Republican Women, Federated. The majority of the 3rd Senate District fell within the Northern Division of Republican Women, but at least it was easier for us to establish rapport with these clubs as we visited them.

Gil had a great deal of charm with the ladies. He made an excellent presentation for Law and Order, but this was his only issue, and the women were concerned with many others. Clare could handle a broader range of topics. Poor Bill Steele didn't stand a chance. After all, the only forums these candidates really had were Republican gatherings and Bill wasn't quite sure what a 'Republican' really was, or so it appeared. As we were told by some of his neighbors in Nevada County, he had talked about running for Congress, but there wasn't much chance for that in the distract – so he registered Republican and filed for the State Senate. It was quite obvious he knew very little of the principles of the party.

We made our first acquaintance with some of his neighbors

in the town of North San Juan shortly after he filed. A number of irate citizens were 'meeting' at Babe's Bar, which was situated across the street from Steele's ice cream parlor. He had provoked their wrath by writing to newspapers in the cities to invite 'hippies' to come stay in North San Juan. He supported the legalization of marijuana to boot, according to sources within the little community. Apparently a number of off-beat young people read his invitation and came, causing the local people to climb the walls with their behaviors. The topper came when the young people were accused of starting a forest fire that almost got the town of North San Juan. The town people were ready to tar and feather Steele. We got a phone call late one night to invite Clare to a town meeting and he was asked to bring campaign literature for them to distribute. Their ringleader was Mickey Gore, a very strong willed lady who could handle two Bill Steele's with one hand tied behind her back if they got out of line in her bar. Clare agreed to attend. Richard 'Smitty' Smith drove up with him. When they returned, Clare was shaking his head in wonder, and Smitty was rolling his eyes eloquently as they related quite the tale.

Mickey Gore had been busily re-registering most of the local Democrats to the Republican Party, and they were doing so for one reason....to vote again Bill Steele. As is the case in many small towns in the hills, the local bar is the unofficial town hall, so a candidate must be able to accept this as a face and be able to handle it. In this case, the meeting that evening was through an archway from Babe's Bar, and lest you get the wrong impression, all of the people attending were not necessarily regular patrons of the other side of the building. It was a regular old fashioned rip-snorting town hall meeting with a complete cross section of the area: businessmen, lumbermen, ranchers and of course, some drinkers and some non-drinkers. Clare presented his reasons for running and described the kind of campaign he intended to wage, which meant a fight minus tar-and-feathers. Whether Bill Steele realized it or not, he might have been treated much more badly if Clare had invaded his stomping grounds to fire up the volunteers for his own candidacy. Later, at a Republican gathering, Steele mentioned, in an aggrieved tone, "Why I wouldn't think of going into your home town, Clare." We personally had no animosity towards either of the candidates and soon realized what a jump we were getting on the Democrat opponent. He was still in session and necessarily spending his days in the Capitol, hitting the trail on weekends, all the while Berryhill was getting established as a bona fide person up in the hills. No easy task for a 'flat-lander' as we in the valley are dubbed. At any rate, Clare was welcome in North San Juan.

We were aware that Steele had married an Asian woman while overseas, and were told that she ran his ice cream parlor. We hadn't met her yet, and had only met Gil's wife once or twice, which was no surprise after he had told Edwina and myself how he felt about women. Someone must have mentioned to Bill that the voters would like to meet his wife, and he found a unique way to 'introduce' her, and gave his own background in about five minutes time.

The time Bill and Gil visited the Stanislaus County Central Committee was when we were absent, as mentioned previously, but our friends present that night couldn't wait for an opportunity to tell us about the evening. Gil and Bill were present in Clare's home county to make their pitch for political support. Gil gave his usual dry, law-and-order routine, and then it was Bill Steele's turn. One thing about Bill, he had a certain flair for the dramatic that was entertaining even if it did make him look the fool.

In the private meeting room of the restaurant where the Central Committee was meeting as usual, Bill arose and with a flourish, placed his Marine's hat on his head, planted an American flag in the center piece, turned on a tape recording of the Marine's Hymn full blast, and turning towards the wall, he unfurled a large poster of his Japanese wife, taken many years before. His wife was dressed in a traditional kimono, a lovely pose underneath a flowering cherry tree. He said, "I understand some of you don't know much about me." It had to be one of the funniest and most unusual presentations by a candidate in their recorded history. He had to be a very frustrated man, but the fact of the matter was, he didn't appear to have principles, political savvy, or much else going for him.

Gil was another matter, as he had some bona fide support throughout the district, and he was a hard working candidate. He also had some formidable troops, so to speak, in the several counties within the district that he served as a commander of the highway patrol. No matter how strongly the public may feel about law and order as a topic of importance, the American people are leery of a strong military or overly authoritarian leader. It just makes the impression of too much of a dictatorship. We had gained a certain respect for the man's abilities, but he came on so strong that my kids nicknamed him 'Colonel Clink', and thus he remained for the entire campaign. I lived in dread of calling him that in public, but it never happened.....I hope. We suspected that even some of his seeming support from the patrol was not bona fide. In fact, we were given reason to believe it was very lukewarm.

Our kick off in Calaveras County, Stokes home ground, was in the historic and lovely old town of Murphy's, at the elegant old Murphy's Hotel. By now we had the motor home and were able to take some of our key workers from Stanislaus up with us for the luncheon. We took the long way up, via Sonora on highway 108, where we got the motor home signed. We then wound north on Highway 49 to Murphy's. Around fifty people were there, which was a highly satisfactory turnout, and the afternoon was a lot of fun. Clare and I leisurely strolled through the small downtown area, and were surprised to find an old school chum of mine, I.N. Berry, holding down the fort as local druggist. The town holds a great deal of charm, and anyone visiting there might be enticed to stay forever. It was still a pleasant surprise to find someone I knew so well that had settled there locally.

At the luncheon we were pleased to see Andy Anderson and his wife, from Vallecite nearby. Andy had at one time been the Republican candidate in the old senate district, and years before he had been a building contractor in Ceres, having built the Ceres Dehydrator for Clare's Dad. Jimmy Oller and his parents were there, from their home in San Andreas, and we were still very close to Jimmy after all of his help for Clare in the previous campaign. His dad, Big Jim, was in a race for Supervisor against Toby Winkler, who was also there and also a supporter of Clare's. One thing about the hills, everyone knows everyone else and candidates had better be a straight arrow, or they are going to be in big trouble!

We left the enchanting town of Murphy's in high spirits, and headed home to get ready to go to the big annual Assyrian dinner in Turlock that evening. Phil and Georgia Paul were the only members of an extremely close family to be members of the Republican Party, and they were such good Berryhill supporters. They held a cocktail party in their home that evening prior to the dinner, and we had an opportunity to meet a lot of new people from Turlock. The Assyrian community in Turlock is a close-knit minority group in an originally Scandinavian town, but they have some common goals. They are ambitious, hardworking, loyal and thrifty. The Scandinavians are strongly Protestant, whereas the Assyrians have their own Catholic Church. So, they share some biases against each other. In our opinion, they have much to make the City of Turlock a very strong town. Most of the Scandinavians are registered Republican, and most of the Assyrians are Democrats. Clare was proud to have a good cross-section of supporters from the Assyrian community as well as the Scandinavians, and that evening was a fun-filled night of dancing, entertainment and camaraderie. We had reached the end of April, and the campaign was in full swing.

Chapter 4 May events

The first of May we were scheduled by Edwina to attend a Republican Women's Club luncheon in Placerville with the other candidates. Gil seemed to have more support here than we noticed in other clubs. Since this was one of the larger counties, we knew we had our work cut out. Both Steele and Stokes were beginning to feel the pressure of a campaign and took this opportunity to strike out at Clare for support that they thought was being manifested from the State Capitol. Clare didn't and couldn't deny that he had personal friends among the legislators, but pointed out that no one resented 'bossism' more than he, nor had anyone been more scrupulous about keeping friendly legislators out of the campaign.

The one exception had been at a dinner in Grass Valley when Assemblyman Bill Ketchum spoke on Clare's behalf. The reason for the exception was the fact that Bill had been a cattle rancher in the area before moving to Paso Robles and getting involved in politics. Since he and Clare had served together on the Assembly Agriculture Committee when Bill was chairman, they decided that this would not be taking unethical advantage. After all, Clare's prior experience as a legislator was a real factor that the other candidates had to deal with realistically.

When the Republican Women's luncheon was over, we went downtown to meet the towns people with Pat Riley, a local Attorney as our escort. Clare felt there was some advantage in having a local person take him around so people would open up a little more freely than they might if you go by yourself. It was a blistering hot day, and we passed on the crosswalk a slightly wilted Captain Stokes, working the other side of the street all by himself.

That evening we got to see Bill Steele's sterling performance with the Marine's Hymn, the hat, flag and poster, when he went through the whole thing in the El Dorado High School library. The TARS, teenage Republicans, had invited the three candidates to speak and after all three presentations had been made, we were pleased to see the young people sign up to work on Berryhill's behalf. Ollio McKenzie, a senior, was Clare's youth chairman, and Oliver never let us down. He and Tom kept in touch for some time after the election.

Our next stop was Placer County, a heavily Democratic registered area, but full of some hard working Republicans that made our acquaintances right away. They not only worked hard, they also could raise money, a constant consideration for a candidate. Members of the Republican Women's Club, which could not take sides in a primary contest, had formed a Couples Club, and, with their husbands, did take a stand for Clare. The Rouseks and the Kibbes hosted a large potluck of this club at the Kibbes home in Hidden Valley, a gorgeous subdivision in the Loomis-Rocklin area east of Roseville. Mike Withers, a mod-appearing extrovert, took it upon himself to whisk us around the room, introducing us to all. He later admitted that he himself was just meeting most of those people for the first time. This nucleus of supporters were involved in every fundraiser and activity Clare had in Placer County.

A couple of days later, Clare paid his first official visit to Auburn, county seat of Placer, as the guest of Wendell Robie. Mr. Robie is a most remarkable elderly gentleman. He was lean and wiry, and he fairly ran Clare's legs off, taking stairways two steps at a time and expounding his patriotic fervor, great depth of character and impressive physical stamina. He still rode the 100 mile trail on horseback yearly that takes place at Lake Tahoe. He had built a successful banking business, and was, indeed, a fine man to have on your side. Clare was tired at the end of the day, but returned home in time for a barbecue put on by the

Stanislaus Country Disposal Association. This was after he had sandwiched in a short stop in Sacramento to discuss copy for 30 second radio spots.

After a much appreciated nights sleep, we went to the Stanislaus County Republican Women's annual May brunch, held in the garden of Maude Lindley's home. Following the morning of relative relaxation with our friends, Clare spoke to the Fidelity Class at the Methodist Church, arranged by Mr. Cooper, his brother Ron Berryhill's father-in-law. Mr. Cooper is a devoted Methodist and Republican, although not necessarily in that order.

It was time to get out and meet some new folks again, so the next day we took off in the motor home with Rae and Smitty for a jaunt to South Lake Tahoe and on up to Plumas County to visit Shirley and Harvey West at Graeagle. As we started to roll up through the foothills towards the towering peaks of the Sierras, we felt the excitement and sense of adventure beginning to build in us. When we reached the summit at Donner Lake we felt giddy with the feeling that anyone who was elected to represent this gorgeous and historical area of California was one lucky fella. Our motor home was a far cry from a covered wagon, but we could empathize with the sense of destiny they must have felt so many years before. It was great to have Rae along, with Smitty doing the driving as usual, so Rae could get a better and more objective sense of the kind of campaign that was developing. The Assembly race had been so entirely different. The motor home was very relaxing, and there was room to move around, stretch out to rest, eat, or make plans.

Smitty was an especially good friend of many years of all of us. We had seen him occasionally when he was at Quigley's as a bartender, but none of us had seen Smitty when he was really in his element. This was the Smitty we met as we invaded Plumas County. He and his wife and two boys had spent every vacation for fifteen years in Blairsden, on the banks of the Feather River. They had explored all of the most remote nooks and crannies of this beautiful river to discover hiding places of the wily trout, and knew all of the back roads like the back of his hand. As we drew near, the usually laconic

Smitty became animated and valuable as he entered his favorite part of the world. No local Chamber of Commerce could have laid it on any thicker. It certainly isn't the least bit difficult to fall in love with Graeagle and the West's, who owned the whole kit-and-caboodle.

The town originally was a company lumber town, eventually put up for sale and bought, along with around 10,000 acres of timber land by Harvey West Sr. His son Harvey and his gorgeous wife Shirley had set out to turn the town into a successful resort and retirement community. They maintained the old company houses in the same barn red and white, but with small businesses or vacation rentals as their destiny now. A lovely 18 hole golf course had been built by Harvey, in addition to two other courses in the close vicinity. t is unpretentious, beautiful and restful. Smitty, sitting quietly on the front steps of the house we were using, solemnly pointed across the street and said, "Rae, you are gonna' run the grocery store. Mer, you can run the gift shop and Clare, you pump gas while I run the bar. We're not going any further." What a temptation.

That evening after a relaxing dinner and stimulating conversation with Shirley and Harvey, Clare gave his best speech, ever. At least a hundred residents of the area were gathered in the community center to hear him. He considers himself a poor 'speech maker', refuses to read a speech, preferring to tell the people how he feels and about his convictions in a conversational manner. He underestimates himself, for the simple eloquence of his presentation touched these people. He spoke of his pride in America, it's great contribution to the people through the free enterprise system, his own love of the land and appreciation for the opportunities afforded the California farmer, in particular, his family's willingness to devote part of their lives to politics. As he closed, his emotions were very close to the surface. The people responded enthusiastically, and a lively time of questions and answers followed. This gave him the opportunity to expound in specifics about his concerns over 'big' government, local control, his low opinion of regional government, and other issues of local concern. I have never been more proud of my husband. Who said he couldn't deliver a good speech?

Gil Stokes flew his own plane into Quincy the next day and we saw him at a pancake breakfast at Feather River College, where we were accompanied by the Carr's, a couple from the community college. His plane gave him an edge over us at times, but we had Max, whom we trusted implicitly as a pilot, when necessary, and there was no comparison to the impact that our bright and cheery motor home had on the folks. On the back roads of the sprawling district, we were spotted and reported to the neighbors as we tooted and waved on our way to the next stop. We had been gathering autographs on the side for several weeks now and they were quite eye catching rolling along the highways and bi-ways. There were some who read our sign, 'JOIN THE BERRYHILL BANDWAGON' and thought we were a rock group! Our mode of transportation was a distinct advantage over the airways when it came to meeting the local people.

For instance, the time we stepped in the tranquil little town of Loyalton in Sierra county, to chat with Hal Wright, editor of the local weekly newspaper. Through his columns, if no where else, people knew where we were and what we were doing. His paper was read throughout the neighboring counties as well. Mait had taught us to respect the power of the local press.

While we were in the neighborhood, we dropped by Russ Turner's picture perfect ranch in Sattley. His log house was nestled against the mountain, with a view across the meadows where his cattle grazed, the lush natural grasses gleaming golden green in the thin spring sun. The snow had melted not so long ago, and all of the streams were full and rushing through meadows towards the rivers. Behind his cattle rose the still snow-capped mountain where his supplemental earning power of Christmas trees contrasted their rich deep forest green. Truly this could be called 'God's Country', and these two young people and their children appreciated this lovely spot where they had both grown up, sharing 4-H experiences as youngsters and now working with their own children. A priceless heritage.

The following day would be hectic for Clare as he and Max were to fly from Quincy to Grass Valley in Nevada County to attend a Cattleman's Association barbecue as the guest of Ivan Branson, his chairman in Nevada County. From there they flew to Martel, a tiny lumber town in Amador County to attend an E Campus Vitus gathering. Flying is not my cup of tea, and naturally I am not a member of the Clampers, so Smitty and I traveled by motor home to meet him promptly at 4 p.m. at Sutter Creek, the nearest town in Amador to the Clampers meeting. We enjoyed the trip down upper Highway 49, detouring for lunch in Downieville, perched on the edge of the Yuba River Canyon. Here, Tom Vilas, Home's cousin, and mayor of Downieville, graciously agreed to sign our motor home, and then we rolled on down the road, stopping once to take pictures of the magnificently breathtaking Buttes. I tried to get Smitty to stop in North San Juan for a beer or a Bloody Mary in the famous Babe's Bar, but Smitty wasn't taking any chances. Nodding a vigorous 'no' to my suggestion, he floor boarded the gas pedal and we careened through downtown North San Juan while saying to me, "No way, Maryellen. For all we know they make the Bloody Mary's with real blood in there. No sir, we're not even gonna slow down". It would be many moons before I finally had the opportunity to meet Mickey Gore in person, that fine, dedicated lady.

Without any further stops, we finally pulled into Sutter Creek, very thirsty and tired. No sign of Clare yet, but Clampers were in evidence all over town. They stood out in their distinctive red shirts, black pants and vests, black hats gaily decorated with assorted buttons and patches from previous outings. This organization is widespread and famous throughout the Mother Lode, as a basically historical organization, devoted to putting up roadside historical monuments and raising hell in general with their parties, usually in that order. Their contribution to sharing the local history with the public is very real, in spite of the somewhat tarnished image some people have of them. It is tongue-in-cheek humor, as they call their chief officer the 'Grand Humbug', gently poking fun at the more dignified fraternal orders. Smitty and I distributed several 'Blondes for Berryhill' buttons, then decided to go into Belotti's bar for a cool drink while we waited for Clare. Much to my surprise, Jack the bartender, disappeared for a few minutes and when he re-appeared he had signed the motor home and announced to all present that he was to be known as one of the 'Democrats for Berryhill'. The Clampers present whooped and hollered and lectured me on the evils of politics until Clare finally got back to town. Then they gave him a friendly going over, too.

Sometime later in the campaign, an ugly rumor circulated about Clare having a drinking problem. I was furious. Anyone who has a problem with liquor would never make it through a primary standing up much less alert and capable of handling the schedule we were following. It was tough enough to do sober.

The next day was Mother's Day and we spent it quietly with Mother, Aunts and just plain family. It was a welcome respite of reality on this different path we had chosen.

The following days sped by with candidates confrontations in Nevada County and Diamond Springs, El Dorado County, where the candidates and the folks met in the Lions Hall for dinner and a chance for each candidate to speak. Gil and his wife were there, but we were beginning to see signs that more of the local people seemed to be lining up behind Clare. From the very beginning, Clare had directed his attack against the Democrat candidate, avoiding hard feelings among the Republican ranks. Bill Steele had to be a very lonely candidate with his various and sundry opinions that were most anathema to Republicans.

However, Law-and Order issues were certainly valid with our audience, so Gil was still in there running hard. Over and over again the people asked, "How do you feel abut gun control?", and over and over again Clare reiterated his belief in the right to bear arms. So did Gil.

We accepted an invitation to a potluck dinner and candidates night in Mountain Ranch, Stokes home town. Rae, Clare and I drove up in the car, leaving early in the day so we could enjoy the scenery leisurely, also allowing ourselves time to find Mountain Ranch which was located far off the beaten track. We were so glad we did, for May in the foothills, after a wet winter, is breath-taking and beautiful with the tall, lush green grasses, wildflowers painting the hills orange, pink, purpose and white. The horses and cattle were also exchanging their rough winter coats for sleek, shiny ones. A sense of renewal is in the air, and while we didn't know what we were going to be getting into that evening, we surely did enjoy the getting there.

Mountain Ranch is a tiny hamlet, but the Community Center was bulging with people and the tables were piled high with a rich variety of food. Tossing caution to the wind, we ate and ate and ate. The evenings program began and Clare turned out to be the only Senate candidate, as Gil apparently felt he didn't need to cover this base. He missed out on a very informative meeting, as candidates for local office presented their differing opinions on issues to the hundred or so people present. Maybe because life is less complicated socially and business wise in the hills, those people really care. They come to meetings where they can hear and be heard in return, and they go to the polls and vote. That evening was 'grass roots' politics at its finest, and we left with a great sense of our faith being renewed.

Chapter 5 All Over the Map!

A week later we went from Placer County for a Republican Women's luncheon with the candidates to Somerset in El Dorado County once again, for a candidates dinner at the Pioneer Union School. Mrs. Peart made all of the arrangements, and again as we wound up a circuitous foothill road, we wondered if people would show up after our hard day of driving. However, when Mrs. Peart decides to help you, you can depend on being helped. Another great potluck, visit with the folks and weary trip back to the ranch. In spite of fatigue, we were filled with a great deal of gratitude for the many doors that had been opened to us by so many willing people.

There is no room for political cynicism when you constantly deal with people like we had been meeting. It was a weary pair of Berryhills that collapsed in their own bed that night in order to rest up for the annual Turlock Chamber of Commerce Centennial Parade and Rodeo the following day. Arrangements were made by Bill Noda, Clare's committeeman in Turlock. Bill and his wife Esther worked hard on Clare's campaign, never taking credit for their many efforts.

The band's hay wagon was ready and waiting and the gang received their usual enthusiastic reception on the parade. It was again a nice feeling to be in territory where we could look around and really know so many people. Most of our encounters had involved a first time meeting and it would take some time to get all of the new friends sorted out of the district we crisscrossed back and forth, up and down. We cut our visit short in Turlock, however, as Edwina had scheduled a busy Sunday. The next day Clare was to be up in Susanville, way up north in Lassen County. She was doing a yeoman's job of scheduling, and had talked to most of the people so often on the phone from headquarters in Ceres that she felt like she really knew them.

Accompanied by Harry Sham, Clare attended the Modesto Lions' Club annual breakfast, and then flew to Susanville to take in the annual Junior Rodeo where Julian Mapes took him in tow. Then he and Max flew to Modoc, where Bob Barclay, District Attorney, took over host duties. Bob is a character in a county rather used to lots of expressions of strong individualism, and there was literally no one that they encountered that was a stranger. Meeting up with Max who sat at the airport strip in Cedarville, they flew off into the wild blue yonder to Portola, Plumas County, and another busy day of meeting new people.

Max and Clare made quick and fast friends with a young couple who owned a sporting goods store and tiny beer bar adjoining their business. They not only seemed to know everyone in town, but Jack and Marlys Bones knew how to fish the famous Davis Lake. Max was determined to catch a big one out of those waters, and the Bones were perhaps the key to the catch. Clare had to keep reminding Max that fish don't vote. It's a wonder we ever got either one of them away from that spot.

We had taken a motor home full of Modesto Young Republicans with us to attend a get-acquainted evening with the Amador County YRs with George Ground driving. The rest of us were hashing over what Clare had been up to, and oohing and aahing over the spectacular scenery on the way up from the flatlands. Stokes and his wife were there also, but, as usual, he and Clare were too busy getting acquainted with the people to have any personal conversation.

The next encounter with him was in Modesto at a party our local Stanislaus Yrs had hosted, and we had a chance to meet 'Boots' Warner, Gil's campaign manager from Amador County. We drove them out to the airport after the meeting, and it was the first time since the day of filing that Clare and Captain Stokes had a chance to chat privately. Clare reiterated his premise to back fully Gil's candidacy if he won the primary. Stokes thanked Clare for his word and after a moment of glaring silence, Boots spoke up. He is a rather gruff, tough man on first impression, and after waiting a bit for Gil to say more, said "That's good of you, Clare. Uh, isn't that the way you feel about it if Clare wins, Gil?" "of, of course" said Stokes. I found it mildly irritating that he had to be prompted to return the pledge, and the needling memory of that moment stayed with me. We both felt a warm feeling towards Boots Warner for his perspective nudging of his candidate to be fair. And modest!

Chapter 6 The June 6th Primary

Our next return trip to El Dorado was rather hectic. On the night of the 25th we attended a candidate night at the elementary school in El Dorado Hills, then returned home for the night. We had to return the next day for an old fashioned political rally in Cameron Park, a few miles east of El Dorado Hills, up highway 50. We had to pick up the band and the motor home for this trip, so we put a few more miles on the car, but there was no other way. Tom's band was unavailable at the last minute, so Bill got his friends from Junior High together, who had been most anxious to have a chance to play at one of the campaign shindigs. We loaded half a dozen gangly 8th graders, drum sets and instruments into the motor home and took off for Cameron Park.

The El Dorado Chamber of Commerce had done a fine job of organizing the afternoon and there was a lot of red-white-and-blue bunting draped around the booths and old fashioned bandstand on the edge of the lake. There were lots of candidates, and not too many people, although there was quite a large group of young people who had come to hear Shirley MacLaine, the movie star, speak in support of George McGovern for President.

I had my hands full with Bill and his buddies, who were getting cold feet about their heretofore heralded musical talents, as they saw so many strange faces. Their eyes were caught by the kayaks, canoes and paddle boats that were available for all to enjoy. Before I knew what had happened, they were out on the lake, boisterously trying to dump each other out of their kayaks. Needless to say, they all ended up in the water, and Stewart lost his brand new eyeglasses in the drink. Our band was finally reassembled, dripping wet in their only clothes for the day, and ready to play. They were invited to play up on the bandstand with a PA system, a first for the group. After the initial shock and self-consciousness that hit them, they did a reasonable good job, and the people enjoyed them. We had a fun day, except for the lost glasses.

We were looking forward to a big weekend at home. Edwina and I were getting food organized for our 2nd Berryhill Boosters' Bash, a picnic-type family get together that was to be held at the Turlock fairgrounds. We had so many commitments outside of Stanislaus County, that this was planned so Clare could see as many of his local supporters at one time as was possible. The picnic was to be on June 14th, a Sunday afternoon. Clare and I attended a fundraiser by the Placer County Republican Women the Saturday night preceding the Bash. The Placer women put on 'A Night in Monte Carlo', which was a tremendous success and much fun. We had to drive the long way home afterwards, and were amazed how it no longer seemed like a long way to Placer County.

Early the next morning, Edwina, the Paul's, Georgia and Phil, along with several other volunteers, were helping us get the food ready to be served. I can truthfully say I have never before fixed 100 lbs of potatoes into salad, or shredded quite so much cabbage for coleslaw. The crew had fun working together, but we knew we had worked. People enjoyed the afternoon and I especially enjoyed a chance to sneak into the motor home to visit with an old Republican buddy, Marge Bright from Turlock. She brought me up to date on all of the local gossip and I filled in from our end. Tom's band was once again blasting out 'Kansas City', and 'Sweet Georgia Brown', and their favorites from the group 'Chicago'. During the months preceding the primary there had been no time to visit with old friends, and we really enjoyed the get together.

Tuesday, June 6th rolled around and we had another primary election day to survive. Clare joined Homer in a golf game again, and I kept busy preparing for the evening vigil to be held at our house this time. Homer's family had incurred more than their share of illnesses, so we wouldn't let them do the entertaining this time.

Rae had extra phones at the Ceres headquarters to get returns from the various counties end precincts. We went down to Yori's Grove and voted early, freeing the rest of the day to get ready for the evening. Supporters arrived early out at the ranch and their jubilant spirits affected us, creating a feeling of excitement among us all. Someone recalled Gil telling Clare about how hard he had worked in Stanislaus County and Clare's grinning reply had been, "Gil, no matter how hard you work, this is my home, and these are my folks. They've gone through too much with me to quit now." Now we would know for sure.

The results were slow getting in from all of the distant parts of the giant district, but it was a whale of a victory, with Clare carrying all but Stokes and Teele's home county of Calaveras, and Calaveras was close.

Chapter 7 Placer and Lassen Counties

We were off and running against our old foe, Ernie, and reaching for the opportunity to serve the district we had already learned to love. School was out, the motor home had it's motor running, and giddily full of faith and hope, we were off to the 'carny train', encompassing 12 county fairs and 22 parades. The campaign started and returned to Roseville in Placer County, often. Roseville was the second largest city in the 3rd Senate District, had a heavy Democrat registration and this reflected the strength of the labor unions. Roseville has a huge railroad terminal, the base of the economy for the city, and we were to find it a tough nut to crack. We had met many good supporters in the Republican Party during the primary, and now we would have to concentrate on getting acquainted and accepted by the larger majority of union-oriented Democrats.

We had good friends in Dave and Zeph Rodriguez, young Republicans who were active in the community and seemed to know everyone in town. They had taken their lumps as Republicans from a few local Mexican-Americans who did not understand their party preference. They found it difficult to accept the premise that the Republican Party offered more opportunity and freedom for the individual, and that was what they wanted. Dave and Zeph graciously introduced us to many groups of people in Roseville, and their children pitched in to help too.

We attended more events in Roseville than any place, starting with the annual Machinists Union Dinner-Dance at Johnson Hall at the fairgrounds. It was billed as a western type evening, so I spent quite some time trying to decide what to wear.

Jeans? No. Just casual? Too blah. Finally I remembered a patio dress that had a patchwork skirt and drawstring peasant blouse, which seemed to fill the bill. When we arrived, I nearly backed out the door before I got all of the way in. The very first women I saw had on elegant long gowns, fur coats, and I was evidently under dressed. Clare said, "It doesn't matter," (typical male attitude), and in we went. We were greeted by Dave and Zeph, and I didn't have time to worry about my dress any more, as they saw to it that we met many people. They arranged for me to draw the prizes and Clare had donated some wine, so we seemed to get along fine on our first evening in their town.

A week or so later we repeated the evening with the Knights of Columbus, again at Johnson Hall, and again the Rodriguez' introduced us to a whole separate group of people, with a few there from our first evening which made us feel at home. We met a lot of Democrats in Johnson Hall, and one evening we were invited to go up to the local Elks Hall to meet a few more. Clare fit in just fine, as he was a member of over 20 years in good standing with the club. His opponent had introduced legislation that would have been very detrimental to the organization, in spite of the fact that he was also a member. At that time, not a very popular one.

That June we also had two graduation ceremonies back in Ceres. Lynne graduated from High School, and Bill from the 8th grade. Now that school was out, Betsy was home from Cal Poly, San Luis Obispo, and more than eager to get in on the campaign. The boys were getting their band together and spending many hours in our living room practicing. My family had been expanded to include the drummer, Dale Goehner, whose family had moved out of town. Dale came complete with drum set, a set of weights for lifting, and earphones and stereo so he could practice two hours a day without other noises distracting. We rather needed our own earplugs, but got used to the practice. There was no doubt that the boys would be a great asset throughout the district fairs, as well as the many parades.

It would be a unique way to involve not only our own young-sters in the nitty-gritty, but also a wonderful opportunity to get other newly franchised voters involved in politics.

The girls and I spent many hours planning with the boys how we would operate in these new towns. We were getting supplies lined up, such as brochures, balloons, litter bags, and comfortable walking shoes. We were also trying to find yellow shirts for the boys in the band to wear along with their straw hats and kelly green vests we made with a yellow felt applique of the district. They could get along with their blue jeans and tennis shoes, so the expense was minimal. The girls added their own bit of atmosphere with long green and white checked skirts, white blouse and yellow pinafores. They learned to hate those outfits before we were through, but they did add a spark to our booth at each fair, and on each of our parade floats.

Our many new friends from the primary were all revved up and ready to go. The Walkers from Auburn, the Rouseks, Kibbes, Withers, Davis' and all of the many couples who we had met at the first, were willing and able to help us campaign creatively.

Wes Sawyer had contacted his many friends in the cattle industry throughout the district and we had some outstand-ing workers in Sierra county with the Russ Turner family in Modoc, with Don Fleurnoy and Bru Christianson (until he was appointed head of the Department of Agriculture by Governor Reagan), and Plumas, where Shirley and Harvey West, Vad-ney Murray and Bob Dellinger did the honors. They helped set up personal appearances, wagons for parades, organized fund-raisers and precinct workers. They also introduced Clare to each local newspaper editor, who, as we knew from past experience, were one of the keys to success. These people are close to the local problems and always proved to be very interesting and in-fluential people.

Wes opened the first doors for us in Lassen with Julian Mapes, a most interesting cattleman. He is a ruggedly inde-pendent cowboy, who had no use for the town folk except in a few rare instances, and felt that if Clare met the cattlemen, he had met all he needed. Unfortunately, Lassen had a poor track record for electing Republicans, and we would have to work long and hard to make any dent in the strongly Democrat town of Susanville.

Tom Sawyer, Wes' son, and I will never forget our first trip with Clare in the motor home, to Susanville. Julian was to meet us in the bar of the Mount Lassen Hotel, where everyone seems to meet, from cattlemen to wives to their children. We were a bit early, so I had a drink while waiting for Julian, and Clare managed to start up a conversation with some of the fellows at the bar. They had sun-tanned, weathered faces, cowboy hats and boots, and were obviously people he could relate to, easier than some. They got into a few dice games for drinks at the bar, and Tom and I sat back in utter satisfaction, and watched as Clare won game after game. He came over to us after about a half an hour, during which time Julian had arrived, and said, "I can't quit now. I've got to lose once and buy these guys a drink, or I sure am not going to make too many friends around here." Julian just grinned and said, "you're doin' just fine, Clare." He sat back with Tom and me and watched a real marathon of a dice game, which Clare finally lost. Again, smiling with no little pride, he reiterated, 'did just fine, Clare, just fine." I guess Julian was correct, for Clare made some lasting friendships that afternoon and I got to meet some of the wives and children that are certainly included in my list of favorite people. 'When in Rome, do as the Romans do' is not bad advice for political candidates. We did meet one city person that same evening after a Farm Bureau dinner that netted five people, including Tom, Clare, and me. Unfortunately for us, there was a Candidates Night for City Council and School Board candidates elsewhere in Susanville that same night, and most people were at that meeting.

However, a young man from high school, wearing a black trench coat appeared, and told us he was interested in meeting the candidate for the Senate. Even though he and his family were Democrats, he thought it would be interesting to meet the Republican candidate. He seemed to be a very serious young man, so Clare spent quite a bit of time talking with him, and we offered to give him a ride home in the motor home since it was a piercingly cold night. He got a kick out of that, and his mother must have wondered 'What on earth?' when we pulled up before their house. The young man's name was Jimmy Chapman, and his father was a teacher at the local community college. His mother was active in Democratic circles, and eventually, Jimmy was elected to the city council. That night we only knew we were giving an interested kid a ride home. It turned out that LaCoste had offended Mrs. Chapman when she gave a coffee for him, and she had no use for him from then on, which didn't hurt us a bit. Clare's opponent managed to alienate people now and then, and we just happened to mosey along at the right time to pick up the pieces.

Chapter 8 Placer County

The first of the fairs was in Roseville, and as a result of all of those nights at Johnson Hall along with the Republican meetings we had attended, we knew more people than we had imagined. We had the motor home strategically placed on the grounds, to serve as our booth, replete with balloons, brochures, etc.

To start the day there was a parade, and we had our truck, hay, band, local youngsters and kazoos for them to play along with the band. It promised to be a scorcher, so we had an ice chest full of ice and coolers of lemonade for the band. You get awfully dry playing those instruments. We were concerned over Danny Talbert, in particular, who had volunteered to play the trombone with us. Danny was a very big boy, and well over 200 lbs. With predictions of 112 degrees for the day, we knew Danny would need plenty of liquids. Tim Fuji had come along to play his trumpet with Tom, so we had plenty of sound. Those boys, along with Doug, Dennis and Dale, had played together all through school In addition to their Dixie and Jazz, they occasionally broke into the strains of the Manzoni Requiem by Verdi, which had been their crowning achievement with Bert Stevenson's band at Ceres High School.

The parade lasted two hours, with the usual delays, and it was sizzling on the hot pavement. The kids went through the ice and the lemonade, and we kept buying them snow cones to help alleviate the discomfort. By the time we reached the fairgrounds, two miserable hours later, Dan and his tuba barely made it off the truck. A gardener saw his plight, and turned the hose with which he was watering the yard, directly on boy and horn. Dan didn't care how wet he was or how bedraggled, but it did dampen his spirits for our parade schedule. He and Tim had played with us the time before at the Apricot Festival in Patterson, but that is a much shorter parade route. The fair got off to a slow start because of the unbearable heat, but we were glad to have a slow day after that morning.

Sally and Oscar Holt had come up with an idea to use campaigning, and had decided to try it out as they visited the Roseville fair with us. They ordered small lapel buttons that were bright yellow and said 'Berryhill Booster'. They gave them out to people who signed up to help and part of the help would be to find five more 'Berryhill Boosters', thus spreading the personal involvement of more people into active participation. We first tried this approach at the small community of Rough and Ready in Nevada County. Rough and Ready was a town of some fame for having attempted to secede from the Union during the early days of California's history; part of the Wild West. Vivacious, redhead Sally quickly made friends and found supporters for her cause. Success under their belts, the Holt's were ready to tackle Roseville.

People were staying away from the fair the first night after the blistering heat of that day, so we were able to visit at greater length with those who did show up. Sally charmed most of our visitors into signing up for her Berryhill Boosters Club, and we could see many folks wearing the bright buttons before the evening was over. The band had attracted friendly crowds who viewed our large bulletin board adorned with pictures of the campaign up to then. We were glad when closing time rolled around, as it had been a long day. We loaded up into two cars and headed for the hotel where we were all staying that first night. I rode with Oscar and Sally. After ending up on the wrong freeway three times, (as it is easy to do in the Sacramento area), we finally joined the gang at the Inn. Crowded into a room with our daughters, we put in a miserable night since the air conditioning wasn't working. The heat wave had put too much stress on the city's power, and we felt one of the first results of the 'energy crunch'.

The remaining days of the fair were fun, with large crowds and we had the opportunity to get better acquainted with some of the people we had met at the dinners in Johnson Hall. Oscar had a little fun with our rival. As candidate 'X' was pressing the flesh on each person who came within striking distance in front of his booth, Oscar eased himself in the crowd, and soon was greeted. Ernie grabbed his hand to shake and presented him with one of his cards, saying mechanically, "Hello....my name is Ernie LaCoste and I'm running for the Senate and would appreciate your vote." Oscar gave his engaging grin and said, "Well hi, Ernie. Wondered where you were keeping yourself these days. How you been?" He said enough to get LaCoste's attention, and Ernie studied him puzzled to have someone in Roseville seem to know him that well, as most people just took the card and kept moving. For the life of him, I don't think he ever put Oscar-Turlock-Berryhill together because then Oscar asked him how he felt about the McGovern presidential candidacy, which had just occurred at the Democratic convention. LaCoste blustered a bit and claimed that he was running an independent campaign and was not involved in the presidential Race. Oscar came back laughing, and we noticed Ernie watching the four of us later in the evening, still not quite placing the Holts.

The first Saturday in July was the date for the annual Apricot Festival in Patterson, featuring a parade and chicken barbecue. Both candidates for the Senate and also the Assembly candidates, John Thurman and Ray Simon, would be making appearances. Clare and I were to ride in a gorgeous Pierce Arrow, vintage 1920, while the band and Smitty with the girls were in the motor home.

As the usual jockeying for position in the parade route took place, we found ourselves in an excellent starting position, while the opposition argued futilely that he was the present Assemblyman and therefore deserved a better spot. One really must be 'into' campaigning to appreciate the significance and satisfaction of one-upmanship involved in these matters. We retained our good spot, and when the band realized they were being shown up by an extra entry by the opposition, they simply drove through the parade route twice, music pouring from the open windows and the girls waving enthusiastically to the crowd. Clare and I were astonished to see them again, since we were finished and were part of the throng lining the street. We all enjoyed the barbecue and our gang had fun with the young people in John Thurman's pep band that had also participated. They were a cute bunch, all dolled up in red, white and blue outfits. Competition among the young people was keen, wholesome and welcome.

Clare or Kim Payne, of the staff, covered many candidate appearances on high school campuses. An important issue with these youngsters was the candidates stand on lowering the drinking age to eighteen. The baby-faced administrative assistant of Assemblyman LaCoste always reflected satisfaction with his statement that his boss was 'for it'. However, when Clare would finish his presentation, the young people might be disappointed but at the same time they seemed to respect him for his honesty. He would point out to them that he had five children, the eldest twenty-one, and his personal feelings as a parent were certainly involved in this judgment. The argument that they listened to thoughtfully was the one that drivers are licensed to drive at sixteen, and have very little experience. To add to this the additional new experience of alcohol seemed to be asking for trouble. He said he didn't want any of their deaths from drunk driving on his conscience. If it appeared on the ballot at some future time he would vote no.

The results of these high school class meetings became quite a 'cause to celebrate' when some of the students got under the skin of LaCoste's administrative assistant and he rudely lost his temper. During a question and answer period some of the youngsters backed him into a corner. At a meeting at another high school the day or so before he allegedly gave Clare's voting record as Assemblyman as being a 'do-nothing' legislator and painted a glowing picture of his boss' own record. Berryhill had a hard core of supporters in each of the schools and word spread like wild fire, so they were ready and waiting for him at Downy High School. The poorly prepared A.A. tried to bluff once too often, and when the students refused to be ignored and patiently reiterated the question about Berryhill's voting record, he turned on his heels and yelled at them as he was leaving the room. "I don't have to answer any of your questions!" The next day Clare appeared before the same classes, not having heard of the uproar the day before, and when they asked him about his voting record, he mentioned several pieces of legislation that had passed and been signed into law.

During his first term after the special election he was elected too late in the year to author any bills, but had co-authored thirty-six bills that had been signed into law by Governor Reagan, including many that strengthened the hands of the college administrators who had been facing so much violence on their campuses. This year, his first full year in office, he had successfully guided sixteen bills to success with the Governor's signature. One that he was really proud of was a bill to regulate the disposal of liquid industrial wastes, fulfilling a recommendation made in 1968 by a water quality study panel of the State Water Resources Control Board. The goal would be accomplished with no additional cost to the public. There was much talk during this time of the student population being very liberal and radical, but we found a large, strong, informed and vocal group of young people who have strong conservative convictions and will be a most welcome addition to the adult world in a few years.

Clare gained supporters from the faculty as well as the student body during these encounters. They were a minority, but we were grateful. There was no doubt about where the powerful California Teachers' Association stood, for they contributed

$5,000 to LaCoste's campaign, and almost succeeded in a vicious smear attack against Berryhill. This was ironic in view of the fact that Clare had always backed the public school system and had five excellent reasons for having a sincere interest in a successful system. He had served nine years as a school board member, being involved in the difficult transition from separate elementary and high school boards to a unified district, and had served two consecutive terms as chairman of that unified board.

LaCoste had children who had attended parochial schools, while giving lip service to the public schools. The only apparent reason behind this support for LaCoste could be traced to the two candidates differing views on the subject of 'collective bargaining'.

Clare refused to be a 'yes man' to any one or any group, including teachers. We got wind of what was going on when Pat Clark called, almost incoherent with rage at what had transpired at a countywide CTA meeting held the night before, and her conversation with some of the teachers who were in attendance. A newly appointed young and ambitious man had been hired by the county CTA, by the name of Ron Roberti. He told his audience the night before that Berryhill had received $65,000 from the Orange County John Birch Society. This was anathema to most of those in the teaching profession that were in attendance. For an educated body, they never questioned the facts or asked for his source of information. It was a patently absurd allegation in the face of the fact that the Birchers were supporting John Schmitz for President, and didn't have that kind of money. We didn't either! Much less from any one group.

Coldly angry, Clare immediately phoned Mr. Roberti and had a conversation that made me glad that I wasn't the gentleman being questions. Roberti finally admitted that the matter had come to his attention from the CTA lobbyist in Sacramento, Wayne Caruthers, who had never once asked to see Clare in his Sacramento office. After pointing out the silliness of the Birch

Society being able to contribute to him or anyone else, he informed Mr. Roberti in no uncertain terms that he wouldn't accept this large sum from any special interest group and furthermore, if he had that much money to spend, all told he sure would be happy, but he did not. In closing his conversation with the chagrined Roberti, he demanded a retraction and apology which he got, although, all those present at the meeting were never formally told, as had been expected.

There were many teachers who wrote the CTA and asked that their money not be used in political campaigns, which was their prerogative. In time, Clare came to workable terms with Ron Roberti, a young man who learned a lot in a hurry. This biased and intolerant group that he led did not look at the overall records of the two candidates, but with tunnel vision saw only that Clare was adamantly opposed to any so-called 'right-to-strike' or collective bargaining for the teachers.

In spite of the CTA's attempt to discredit Clare, he picked up not only a few loyal supporters among the faculties, but many young people volunteered to help because of what they had witnessed in the confrontations. Their contribution of time and effort was greatly appreciated. Penney Williams and Esther Morrison of Clare's staff, led several successful ventures with these youngsters. They spent several Saturday mornings going door to door with literature, and washing windshields at shopping centers, placing literature under the wiper when they were finished. At noon they would hike back to a nearby park for roasted hot dogs and cold drinks. Clare had no better campaigners.

Chapter 9 El Dorado and Tuolumne Counties

It was like a breath of fresh air to journey to Jackson in Amador County where we attended the opening celebration of their Republican headquarters. Gene Chappie and Hugh Fluornoy were also there from Sacramento. The building was packed with Democrats as well as Republicans, since the support for McGovern, the Democrat candidate, was nearly non-existent. They had a buffet table loaded with a beautiful array of h'ordourves, and carved watermelon baskets loaded with fruit salad, plus an open bar. Clare had none other than Boots Warner as his chairman, with Maureen Crosby as co-chairman. Don Howard served as his Democrats for Berryhill chairman, although it took a long time to convince his beautiful wife Janice that anything good could come out of politics. When their best friend John Begovich had lost in the previous reapportionment race, Janice had most of her worst fears confirmed.

The next morning we were in Sonora, Tuolumne County, with Clare, speaking at a 7 am. Kiwanis breakfast, followed by a walking tour of the telephone company. Laurel Richardson, formerly of Turlock, was our hostess for this tour, a coincidence since she had served in this same capacity in Turlock during the special election! The telephone company does a fine service for both their employees and the candidates by giving these tours, and gives a chance for candidates from both parties to meet the workers.

At the conclusion of our tour of Ma Bell, we took a walking tour of downtown and the Jacobson's laundry with Kim leading the way in his home town, then drove out to Columbia to the Stevenson home. We had a delightfully relaxing time at their reception, enjoying the view of their garden and pond with mallard ducks placidly floating by and flowers abloom everywhere. Kim was well liked by the people in Tuolumne County and we saw another side of this personable young man. We had been impressed by his ability to stand up to LaCoste's A.A. at some of the high school encounters, in spite of the fact that he may have felt uncomfortable explaining Clare's stand against lowering the drinking age to 18. His mod hair, busy mustache, and common sense approach made him very appealing to all ages.

Our next stop was El Dorado County for the fair held in Placerville, or 'Hang-town', as it is known from gold rush days. We looked forward to spending a few days here, and the boys got a break when Dick Moss invited them to spend the nights at their house instead of in the motor home, as was usually the case. They were most grateful, for whatever else it may be, that motor home never became 'home sweet home' to any of us. One evening when the band was going strong and a large group of listeners had gathered, we took off down highway 49 for Columbia once again. We didn't like to leave the motor home without an adult in charge, so cousin Ester and her husband Tom drove up from Sacramento to hold down the fort. June and Bob Davis drove over from Placer County to help run our 'booth'. We really appreciated their help, and they said they had a nice time. t is really a fun fair, with many, many craft booths full of interesting merchandise and fascinating young people.

The barbecue in historic Columbia was to raise money for the Cancer Drive encompassing both Stanislaus and Tuolumne Counties. It was one successful event, for sure. People were lined up for two blocks for the pit barbecue, with tantalizing odors wafting to your nostrils as the line wound slowly to the busy servers. The wait was not boring, since several groups of musicians took turns playing a variety of music. There were Dixie land groups, guitar and singers, Honky-Tonk piano, old time fiddlers and folk dancers putting on one long and continuous show. Everyone was decked out in western clothes and in the mood for a festive evening. No one was disappointed. Perhaps the secret weapon for America to continue to sustain it's generous spirit is the volunteer organization, whose workers raise so many millions of dollars for worthy causes such as the fight against cancer.

As we wound up the twisty, unbelievable road from Columbia to Angels Camp, we had a nice warm, rosy glow inside because of the spirit of the evening. In no time we were back in Placerville. Dale was resting after several hours of arduous work on his beloved drums, and we knew he was tired for he was allowing some local boy to take a turn, to a large appreciative audience. We thanked our friends for helping, gathered up our daughters' and headed for the motel, noting with satisfaction that the old opponent had already turned in for the night. Quite often we found ourselves staying at the same motel, and we always considered it an extra for the day when we might start earliest and finish last.

The boys were enjoying their stay in real beds at the Moss house, and only one night did they have to make their own way to their benefactor's house. The next day we found out why Dick had shown up to drive the boys home. He had an unplanned delay when he approached the Republican Women's booth, a trailer, to take in the posters, as he did each evening. Three young, strapping mountain boys, who had a few too many beers decided to rip off Nixon's poster. Now, Dick Moss is a big man himself and in pretty good shape after many years in the U.S. Army, so he took the boys measure, and decided that with three of them, no matter how inebriated, he had to consider his age, and had better have one punch do the job of three. He hauled off and decked the first one that came at him, and that was the end of the fight. The young man was delivered to the hospital with a very sore jaw, and the buddies sobered up in a hurry. Dick was a bit concerned that his lawyer was out of town, but perhaps the boy had had all they wanted for that was the end of the subject.

By the end of the week when the fair closed with the dramatic and exhilarating arrival of the annual Wagon Train to the fair grounds, we were feeling quite at home. The boys were all sporting beautifully handcrafted leather belts from the nearby booths, and the girls were carrying new leather purses that would last them for years. We were so sorry that Betsy had come down with a miserable summer cold and had stayed with her Grandmother the entire week. We arrived home, cooked for the week, loaded the motor home with one and all and headed for Quincy, Plumas County, beginning to feel like real 'Carney' people, in a routine that was becoming second nature.

Chapter 10 Plumas County

We arrived in Quincy, hot, tired, and with additional dirty clothes that had been overlooked in our quick transition. We were warmly welcomed by Vadney and Jean Murray along with Bob and Lucy Dellinger, Clare's campaign chairmen. The laundry was quickly whisked into their washers and driers. We found our motel reservations in a delightful spot positively brimming over with colorful petunias, and knew that we were going to enjoy our stay in Plumas County. The boys had parked the motor home at the fairgrounds and had gotten permission to stay there at night. Big John, the hot-beef-sandwich man was next to them again, and the spot was near the rodeo arena where crowds gathered for the evening shows, so the exposure would be good.

The Dellingers had a lovely quiet family barbecue for us with their next door neighbors, the Murrays, and everyone relaxed and enjoyed it before we drove over to the fairgrounds to take in a unique show for a county fair. They were presenting a local cast in the operetta, 'The Pirates of Penzance'. We were really looking forward to the show, since we were acquainted with the airport manager from Beckworth, Frank, who was one of the choir members. We had a mutual friend in Harry Sham, who had taught Frank to fly, and had soloed him in March, 1936. Coincidences such as this tended to create a more believable, smaller scale to the overwhelming dimensions of this district we were tackling.

Smitty, fishing pole in hand, had quickly headed for his favorite 'glory hole' on the Feather River, so the kids were on their own with our 'booth', while we attended the shows. We arrived at our seats for the operetta and shortly after it started we heard the very familiar strains of 'Kansas City' wafting on the breeze from our pep band, and nearly drowning out the voices from the 'Pirates of Penzance'. Some way to make friends and influence people. Quickly we sent a youngster running over to the band to tell them to 'cool it' until the musical program was finished.

Saturday morning was the parade. Vadney and Bob had a wagon and hay lined up and we wrapped our 'Join the Berryhill Bandwagon' banner around the bottom of it, piled it full of local youngsters to play our kazoos along with the pep band. The girls appeared fresh and charming in their gingham pinafores. We enjoyed one of the friendliest crowds, and enjoyed a fine position in the parade, breaking up in laughter as we came to the end of the route. The crowd was beginning to break up and head for home, while the LaCoste camper was still in line waiting to start, with Barry, the A.A. in a rage. Another coincidence had been in old Modesto Jr. College buddy, now a resident of Quincy, who was in charge of the parade. He and Max were waiting to fly Clare to a barbecue elsewhere, and they were standing on the corner, doubled up laughing like a couple of kids over their coup in the parade line-up.

The schedule was getting more and more hectic, but at least some semblance of routine had evolved. When Clare came to town, he would be escorted by his chairman through the business district, often speaking to a men's service club or a Republican organization. The kids and I would spend our days going door-to-door with literature. In Quincy, we were chased off by quite an assortment of angry dogs, and one bit of trivia we acquired was which town enforced leash laws and which ones didn't. The big boys would cover one area, and Janie, Bill, Lynne, Betsy and I would cover another. We girls maintained a healthy respect for the local canines, but Bill, had his share of memorable moments. One large shepherd type, obviously a LaCoste supporter, put us in the car in a hurry, but Bill stood his ground until the last second, when campaign literature flew up in the air and all over the street as Bill did a record sprint to the car. Most of the people kept fences around their houses, but this was never made clear to us – was it to keep the dogs in, or the dogs out? It kept us nimble.

We reluctantly left the warm hospitality of Plumas County carrying with us fond memories and a couple of more tangible reminders. Betsy and Doug had purchased genuine buffalo skin jackets at the fair. As we flew off we adopted the slogan for our time in the sky. I am a fearful flier, trusting no other pilots like I trusted Max, and even with him I was uneasy until I recalled the Psalm 121: "I will lift mine eyes to the hill whence cometh my strength." As the self appointed chaplain of the Berryhill Air Force, I found much comfort in that verse, and found it doubly significant when we considered the fact that our greatest strength in the voting public might also be those staunch friends we had made in the hills.

Chapter 11 Tuolumne County and 'the Cabin'

The weather in Quincy had been very warm, but as we moved on to the Sonora fair in Tuolumne County, it became scorching once again, reminding us of our first fair in Roseville.

The day before starting our Tuolumne schedule we returned to Modesto for a very special event. The members of the building trades had a fundraising golf tournament for Clare. What made it remarkable was the fact that this particular group had never backed a Republican candidate publicly before, west of the Mississippi River. However, Clare's candidacy and his opponent's arrogant attitude had promoted this action. Some members were frightened off from supporting Clare because of threats from our opponent of retaliation when they would get elected, but most members got their backs bowed by this attitude. They were told that if they participated, no bill of interest to the building trades would get to first base. In this day and age of environmental impact planning, there are many issues before the legislature affecting the many lives and jobs of people involved in building. We were proud of those determined friends who plowed on getting the gold tournament organized. They realized that the time had come when the voters simply must analyze the man, not just his party affiliation.

Perhaps underlying our whole line of attack was this basic belief that Berryhill was the better man for the job. The legislature has a crying need for men from a variety of backgrounds to help make decisions for the state. Even with a victory on Clare's part, the California Senate would still be heavily weighted with 21 lawyers. The men of this profession can still maintain a private practice while serving in office, while it is most difficult for a businessman to jeopardize his business to enter politics; or a teacher, or a doctor. It is also difficult for someone in agriculture, but our ranch was at a good point in it's development to allow Clare to take the time to participate in his adventure. Agriculture surely had been good to us, and we needed a strong voice in Sacramento. They needed more than one, but you have to start somewhere. We really appreciated this expression of trust by the men in the building trades. t took courage to do what they were doing, and maybe some good for the future of politics will occur because of their determination to work for the man, not the party.

We joined the troops in Sonora, ably chaperoned by Edwina while we were in Modesto. It was hotter than blazes, but the band was going strong when we arrived and I noticed the usual number of cute girls who had volunteered to blow up balloons for us. It gave them a good chance to flirt with Dale. Our drummer attracted bevies of pretty teenage girls wherever we went, and we always enjoyed his unique contribution to the work. Balloons were a popular item to give away. Even the boys in the band, with their excellent lung power and breath control, were hard put to keep up with the demands of the balloon customers. For a brief time while we were in Nevada County, Doug brought a gasoline driven motor to make their job easier, but the amount of noise and fumes this monstrosity created relegated it to the back of the bus. We envied Assemblyman Gene Chappie and his aid on the campaign trail, Ben Scheible, who had a pump that shot out balloon after balloon. Such is the life of the rich and famous, we decided. At any rate, Dale and his 'crew' were hard at work blowing up balloons and attaching them to long sticks. We were pleased and surprised to see a young Republican couple from Modesto assisting the kids.

John and Vicki Hollis had decided to take a drive up to see

how we were doing. They were instantly put to work on the balloon brigade. They manned the booth while Edwina and I drove on over to Columbia to get settled in Nancy and Hank Haber's mountain home that they had graciously offered us to use while we were at the Tuolumne County fair. It was a darling house nestled in the pines with wild blackberries, three bedrooms, and ample room for everyone to stay together for a change. The boys wouldn't have cooked in the motor home at the fairgrounds, because an intense heat wave had hit and temperatures were soaring from 105 degrees upward to 110.

The fairgrounds were in a little valley on the edge of Sonora where very few breezes could reach. We were also including Ben Scheible in our group. He was all by himself, a rather lonely job for a gregarious, college boy, and we all enjoyed Ben. He was an extremely bright boy with the curious political itch that somehow infects many of us, and this job would, he hoped, open political doors for him at some later date. I hoped it would.

So, we had to get food for Dennis, Doug, Ben, Bill, Tom, Dale, Betsy, Lynne and Janie plus we three adults. Edwina had also made arrangements with Bert Stevenson from Ceres to fly up and pick Clare up on Saturday morning, delivering him to South Lake Tahoe, where he was to join up with the gang coming out after the annual Jeepers Jamboree. All seemed to be going well and the folks treated us with great friendship and hospitality. The cabin had a fan that kept the air circulating and we felt like we were in 'hog heaven', but naturally, not for long. The water quit. Then the fan quit. The only thing that didn't quit was the dirty dishes. By dinner time, Edwina and I were ready to quit, too. The next morning, without even a cup of coffee to bolster our sagging spirits, we took Clare over to the airport to meet Bert. Janie had gotten up early, so she could tag along to see her beloved band teacher rescue her lucky Dad. As he dashed for the plane, he turned, waved, and said, "Sure hate to leave you gals and that mess, but you'll think of something". With his big grin he soared off into the 'wild blue yonder'. Wina and I looked at each other with dismay. Saying not one word, she drove us to the nearest restaurant and the three of us ate a gigantic, delicious breakfast, and vowing secrecy, we returned to the cabin and our latest condition of chaos. Ben was wandering around with a mouthful of toothpaste waving a toothbrush and saying "shiliniglwbr," or something like that. Resourceful Edwina thought of ice cubes, and Ben was saved.

Kim and his friend, the Jacobson boy, whose parents owned the laundry we had visited, assured us that they would get things fixed, and sent us off to the fair. That night we got back to our same problem, but were too tired to care. We all fell in bed early, and were instantly in the deep sleep of innocent babes. In the middle of he night Janie, Edwina and I were awakened from this lovely sleep by Betsy and Lynne knocking on the wall in-between our rooms and Betsy loudly whispered, "Mom, there's a bear in the cabin!" Holy jumpin butterballs, I muttered to myself crossly, and then all of a sudden wide awake. I sprung into action. At last I jumped out of bed, and then common sense stepped in and helped me decide not to open the door. By this time Betsy was going, "psst, psst" to the boys out on the sleeping porch, finally getting them all awake and aware of the problem. I leaned heavily on the door, partly to keep the bear out and partly to hold me up. Then I recalled that Bill and Ben had put their sleeping bags on the couch, right in the middle of the house where the bear might be at that very moment. The boys started hollering and pounding around with sticks and soon they yelled, "All clear". We came stumbling out of the bedrooms. Betsy will never live this down. As she told the story, she heard a bag of potato chips rattling which had awakened her and she was ready to come out fighting the boys for waking her up for eating all of the potato chips. She quickly realized that the boys were all snoring peacefully away on the porch and the intruder was definitely a clumsy, noisy fellow, and her fertile imagination told her that it was a bear. When the dust had settled we could see the tracks and knew that it was a friendly neighborhood raccoon. Just what we needed, but far superior to the neighborhood bear. Before falling back into an exhausted sleep I thought to myself, "What is a nice farmers wife like me doing in a place like this?"

Later in the morning, Kim came back and we tried to get the water flowing once again, but to no avail. Kim again assured us that he would take care of it, so with a small prayer to the God of fools and candidates wives, we got back to the fair, closed up the motor home and headed for home. The kids drove my car back to the ranch and Edwina and I headed down in the motor home after stopping at the directors room at the fair to thank them for their hospitality. A great bunch, fair directors, and in Sonora, Clare had a long time friend in Jimmy Pinjaro, owner of a Union service station in town. Jimmy had worked for Clare's Uncle Leonard many years before, and had loved him as we did, and all of those who had known him. Although Jim was a Democrat, I don't believe he ever wavered in his support for Berryhill, and we value that kind of friendship. After our rather hot and harrowing experiences of the past 48 hours, Wina and I decided to stop at Dave Bonavia's fine restaurant in Jamestown and treat ourselves to a good dinner and a big glass of water!

Chapter 12 Georgetown and Amador County

The Berryhill Bandwagon was seen many places, being very visible with it's color and signs, and we tried to make use of this vehicle. For instance, Clare's nephew Mike and his wife Fran borrowed it for a weekend, taking several couples with them to Grass Valley, Nevada County for a Junior Chamber of Commerce convention. People gave us credit for being many places at the same time, which we all know is impossible, but the illusion was apt.

We were getting organized for the fifth annual Georgetown Founders Day parade. Georgetown sits high on a ridge above the American River, south of Auburn and north of Placerville. We were not using the motor home this day and were grateful as we wound up the hairpin turns from Placerville. In cars and our pickup it is a grueling road, and as we came around one curve what did we see but LaCoste's ancient red fire engine out of commission. Barry Wyatt, the A.A. was standing disconsolately beside it, utter frustration on his face. We waved as we drove by, but our smiles were short lived, for after we got the pickup all decorated and the band stuffed into the back, the machine wouldn't budge. After considerable fussing over it, the parade began, and it looked like we wouldn't have an entry either. We finally all got behind and gave it a giant angry push, and it took off, with the band giving out a rousing version of 'Sweet Georgia Brown'. We had our buddies, Jack and Shirley Wherry with us this time, so they could go back to Modesto, and when the next person said, "Is Berryhill doing anything? We never see him.", they could fill in at least one day's activities.

The charm of Georgetown completely captivated them, and we enjoyed the rest of the day, visiting the booths lining the main street. Jack, never one to pass up good eats, purchased a delicious homemade pie for us to have for desert after our picnic. We drove down the easier road to Coloma and after touring the park where Marshall discovered gold, we hungrily ate our lunch and devoured the pie Jack had bought.

The kids made a discovery of their own, much to Shirley and my dismay. Dale, our drummer, and adopted boy for the summer, and Jeff Bell, a Cal Poly student living with the Wherry's that summer, had discovered a young lady giving away puppies. They both couldn't live without one apiece. The Wherry and Berryhill households had been augmented by puppies that were a mixture of black Labrador and Saint Bernard. An expression we had all picked up from Kim came to mind. He would hold up his fingers like quotation marks and his mouth would form one word, "WOW," and that seemed to say it all.

During the following week, Clare and I had what seemed to be an evening impossible to find during a campaign. We attended the band concert in Graceada Park, around the corner from where I grew up in Modesto. One of the musicians had attended a get-acquainted party for Clare in Modesto, and invited us to be his guest if we could work it into the schedule. It was one of those delightfully balmy summer evenings in the valley, so it was comfortable to sit in the outdoor amphitheater and soak in the music. It brought back floods of memories of past years when I had listened to so very many of Professor Frank Mancini's kids make music at that same park. To our surprise, the master of ceremonies very kindly introduced Clare out in the audience, so we hadn't 'wasted' an evening away from the hurly burly of politics, although it was one of the very few really relaxing occasions we had known or would know for some time.

August was upon us, and the Stanislaus County fair just around the corner. First we journeyed back up to South Lake Tahoe to attend a party with friends from the Tahoe area and Alpine country at Bill Johnson's house. Bill and his wife, Felice, were both from pioneering Tahoe families and they opened up their beautiful home to us on several occasions. We enjoyed the chance to visit with old friends, Ralph and Grace King from Echo Summit. Formerly, Grace had lived across the street from Clare's mother in Ceres, so we shared a friendship that went far back before Clare entered the political arena. Ralph was always a loyal Berryhill booster and occasionally got in a good word for his candidate when he called in a weather report to Modesto's local radio station, KTRB. We had to make it a quick trip, though, because 'our' fair was about to get under way.

I had mixed feelings as I realized that this would be the first fair in several years that our children wouldn't be participating in 4-H activities, but then I thought about sweeping 'unga-unga' with Bev Zaumeyer, and got over my nostalgia a bit. As close to the action we would get would be the Junior Livestock Auction, when Clare would purchase a lamb from one of the youngsters. This turned out to be quite a big campaign expense, for even though the animal can be resolve at market price, the inflated prices the 4-H and FFA animals bring, do add up when you must purchase an animal at each fair – and we had 12.

The entire week preceding the fair had been unbelievably hectic, even after thinking we had set as fast a pace as was possible. Jack Welter, political writer for the San Francisco Examiner had followed Clare's campaign in Plumas and Sierra counties for an entire week so he could write a feature story in depth. Clare was plenty tuckered out at the end of that trip. In addition to the usual tours and receptions during fair time, this visit north had been complicated by fearful forest fires nearby. As we went door-to-door distributing our literature, we would be met at the door by exhausted housewives who had just gotten back from a shift of cooking and serving the firefighters. Clare visited a firefighting unit to see first hand this operation, one that local people are all too familiar with in the mountains.

Clare had flown with Max to Martell, down in Amador County to tour the American Forest Mill there, and, then Fat Crosby guided him on a tour of Ione, Jackson and Sutter Creek. They had dinner at Bellotti's with Don Howard, chairman of Democrats for Berryhill in Amador County. When Clare got back to Sierra county, I met him at the Beckworth airport and we hurriedly drove to Sierra City to attend the Fireman's Dance. Jack Welter had stationed himself in Sierra City, hoping to sneak in a little fishing along with the journalism, but at dinner before the dance, he admitted to having little 'spare time'. As weary as we were all becoming, we thoroughly enjoyed the dance in the old wooden building, with the old-timers and the young people attending, the latter wanting to participate in the 'old fashioned' dancing that we all did, but they had never learned the steps. So, they simply joined hands and skipped around the room, having a good time, anyways.

The next morning we went with Vadney Murray and Bob Dellinger to the Quincy fairgrounds to attend their Buyers' Breakfast. I once again distributed our little packets of dried apricots with Betsy's hand printed notes attached that said, "Pick of the crop – Vote for our Dad', and had a campaign card attached. We had taken four days to pick, cut and dry those apricots. Frank and Annalee Dompe from Crowslanding had graciously offered us all we wanted after their trees had been picked for commercial sales. The kids, Edwina and I, picked and picked and picked, with petite Annalee hauling ladders from tree to tree, and Frank urging us to pick some more. We ended up with two tons of fruit. With expert advice from Clare, the old fruit tramp himself, and recruiting every single youngster who came out to visit our kids while we were home those few days, we ended up with some really beautiful dried apricots to distribute at the county fairs. A nice touch, we thought. The people in Quincy enjoyed the treats.

After purchasing another lamb at the sale, Betsy, Clare and I left in our car, while Smitty and the rest took off in the motor home. We found ourselves on the road from Quincy to Bear Valley, in Calaveras County, on August 13, our wedding anniversary. We were all in our clothes that were appropriate for a livestock auction, but not for a formal reception such as we had been invited to at Lou Gremp's Bear Valley home. Betsy and I had laid our long dresses on top of the suitcases in the trunk of the car, along with a suit for Clare, and one corked Clare crawled into the back seat and went to sleep. Betsy and I took turns driving down highways 70 and 39, down through Carson City and Minden, in Nevada, and over the pass to California once again. Our plan, as outlined by chief scheduler, Edwina, was to go directly to Lou's house to change, and we would have a lovely afternoon to celebrate our anniversary, since the occasion was the formal reception for the Bear Valley Music Festival. When we drove up to the house we discovered people in long dresses and suits already arriving for the festivities. We looked at one another in dismay, said nothing, but headed for the nearest service station to call Lou and tell her there was no way we could attend the party. "What? What? It's so noisy in here I can't hear you", Lou yelled at us. "You can't come? Why? Oh dear", she moaned. "There is a big bottle of champagne chilled here for your anniversary." We finally more or less explained our predicament, hung up, got back in the car and Clare said, "Happy Anniversary, honey". As we drove on down the highway, unbidden tears spilled from my eyes.

Chapter 13 Lassen County

The next day or two were spent with Clare busy with meetings close to home while I washed, cooked and packed the motor home preparatory to our assault on Lassen County. This was to be our fourth or fifth trip to Susanville, an area in the district that I especially loved. Every time I got in the country I had the strange sensation of coming home again, and a sense of excitement always filled me. We were certainly looking forward to seeing so many of the friends we had made, such as Mayor Ivor Lanigar, Julian Mapes, Bud and Sue Price, Anne Brines, Verna Maude, Leland Woods and Cecil and Dane Webb.

Clare was whisked off for a visit to the California's Pacific Utilities Company, City Hall and the Court House, along with a business' walk through, followed by an address to the Rotary Club. We did our door to door bit and Bill had another memorable and dramatic encounter with the dogs. Smitty had distributed us from one end of town to the other, and was hard-pressed to remember where everyone was, spread out as we were over this city of 7,000 people. I was standing on the corner of a block I had just finished, admiring the view from this hilltop that overlooked the city, and the miles of open land, gleaming gray and gold in the summer sun. I was thoroughly enjoying a moment of rest, when I glanced around to see Bill heading for sure trouble. He was wearing a campaign paper sunshade and carrying a litter bag full of brochures. A German Shepherd was rapidly approaching from his rear, and another big dog, a black sort of shepherd type tore out of a yard to his left, obviously bent on total destruction of this neighborhood intruder. I screamed at him, and this time he didn't stop to make friends, he just took off, picking 'em up and putting 'em down in world record time. A nice lady who had talked to me a few minutes earlier saw the situation from her front door and gave us a speedy refuge. As we glanced back at the intersection that Bill had just sped across, without looking left or right, we could see that one dog had his paw firmly planted on the visor, and the big black dog was angrily chewing up brochures. We were glad that that had been our last block to cover, and gratefully, we collapsed in the motor home when Smitty finally located us. It had been an interesting day, though, having been recognized by two fellows who had previously lived in Ceres and taught school at Ceres High School. They were now teaching at the beautiful new Lassen High School in Susanville, that had the breathtaking view of Mt. Lassen towering behind it. Somehow, you are always surprised to find someone you know when going door-to-door in a new town. After our initial timidity we had learned to enjoy the personal contact with the voters.

While in Lassen County, we journeyed with 'Uncle Richard' and a young man from Brigham Young University who had volunteered to help go door-to-door in nearby towns. We tackled Herlong first, since Clare had an appointment to meet Colonel Anderson to tour the Army Depot that was the backbone of Herlong. The homes were compacted into neat, short blocks and we covered it in record time. The Berryhill Bandwagon drew much attention in this isolated neighborhood, and Smitty and Dennis started clowning around. At this time we discovered Dennis Cyphers whimsical sense of humor and ability to mimic. He quietly sat by the window watching young and old coming out of their homes to stare at our motor home, probably wondering, as others did, if we were some lost Rock group. Dennis spoke up, in a high pitched nasal twang "Looky thar ma" he drawled, "That's a big green thang out thar and see these holes in it's stomach? It's et some people." He had us laughing for hours afterwards. He, Doug, Dale, and Tom really got put down by one housewife much to their surprise, and mine. When she came to the door she said, "When your father and mother get your hair cut, I will read your literature. You should be ashamed of that long hair." BANG went the door. After they told me, I took a good objective look at them and sort of shuddered. We hadn't been home any day but a Sunday or Monday for a long time and the barber shops were closed then. None of us had given a thought to how long their hair had grown. Maybe they had chosen not to mention it, since the length of hair the kids liked was quite a bit different than what we liked. They got their hair cut pronto, however, after that encounter.

I let the boys take my car and follow Smitty, Betsy and me in the 'Big Green Machine', as we had dubbed the motor home, after Dennis' little act in the streets of Herlong, because I wanted to get in on some of Smitty's tales and so did Betsy. One story in particular carried us through miles of deserted landscape, as he related the 'true' story about a supposedly haunted house in the little town of Markleville, the county seat of Alpine County. Betsy was so delighted with his tale that she vowed to go door to door there, a wish that was never fulfilled, but we certainly had an entertaining and relaxing trip after a rather harrowing experience the day before while still in Susanville at the fair.

Max and Clare flew down to Sacramento to attend a meeting with Senator Harner. It was a day of cold, biting wind, and overcast skies that held the threat of rain or snow. Max had checked and double checked the weather conditions for flying, for he had one motto he flew by, "I'd rather be an old, cowardly pilot than a daring dead one." So, when he judged it was safe to fly they took off for Sacramento, and not before. Take off time was 2:45 and they returned safe and sound, having encountered no bad weather right on time at 5 o'clock. Clare met me at the Mt. Lassen Hotel where a reception for him was already under way. I was very glad to see him, not only because I always feel better when our feet are on the ground, but also because Verna Maude had outdone herself, as usual, on the party arrangement with the room packed. Dale Goehner had forgotten his suede suit, his most valued possession except for his drums, down in Ceres, so Rae Codoni had taken the opportunity to deliver the suit and get in on the campaign. There is no finer place to get in on the action than with this group at the Mt. Lassen Hotel, and Rae had a fine evening with all of us.

About eight o'clock we left to join the girls and boys at the fair where they were in full swing. The band had attracted a crowd, and the girls were busily handing out balloons and brochures, looking fresh as daisies in their gingham dresses and Berryhill straw hats. Since they seemed to have things well in hand, we wandered around the fair, eventually bumping into Ernie LaCoste, looking distraught and lacking his usual air of assurance. He told us about his very frightening day. A young pilot was flying his wife Jeanne and daughter, Debbie, up to meet him. They were two hours overdue and no one knew where they were. We felt so sorry for him, and were greatly relieved to hear after a short time that the plane had landed at Oroville, way off course, but at least they were safe and sound. I thought to myself, Thank God for the 'coward' that flies us.

The next day Clare was to tour the Collins Lumber Mill in Chester and the rest of us were to go door-to-door, as usual. My problem was a ton of dirty clothes and I felt duty call me to the nearest laundry mat. Clare told one of the boys to go do the laundry - he was taking me with him! I jumped at the chance and it turned out to be a very interesting day, hearing the concerns of the community first hand and visiting the downtown businesses for the first time. When visiting with the young couple who had just recently taken over the Sears and Roebuck catalog store, Clare had to drag me away, for we had discovered that we were mutual admirers of the writer-philosopher Ayn Rand, and I could have stayed all day. However, we had to pick up the walkers and the clean laundry and then drive over to Westwood to meet Lewis Timberline and tour the area.

Westwood and Chester are both beautiful and charming

towns, but Westwood was just starting a renewal program in their town which had become quite depressed after the mill there had closed down. They seemed to be on the right track, attracting resort businesses and people who liked the quiet atmosphere and the proximity to Lake Almanor. When we got back to Susanville, Clare went on the radio with Cecil Webb who owned the station. We then had a pleasant dinner with friends at the lovely old mansion that had been restored and was maintained by the Elks club, finishing the evening at the fair with the young people. It had been another long day.

The next day was Saturday, and the streets of Susanville were colorfully decorated and bustling with participants and observers of the annual parade. It wound down the hill of the main street, starting from the Elks Club at the top end of the street. The Elks Club has a tradition of holding a gin-fizz breakfast for those participating in the parade, and everyone gets in the mood for a really fun one. 'Uncle Richard' and the boys weren't in nearly as good a mood as we were when we joined them, for they were having one dickens of a time wrestling with the bales of hay and the ungainly huge banner that had to be hung around the flatbed truck. This truck was a bit different than the others we had used and Doug had a bad attack of hay fever. Tom, Dale and Dennis were hot and disgruntled as they tried to get the drums and chairs arranged on the truck in the searing heat of mid-morning. Once we got under way, the band never played better, and the girls had never looked prettier. Clare and I have never had more fun in a parade, and we were so pleased to win a trophy for our entry, which is proudly displayed in Clare's office.

Later I had the chance to join Sue Price and Verna Maude Wood at the rodeo and watch Bud ride his beautiful buckskin that I had been admiring, cheering him on in the competition. These friends lived in an isolated precinct out of town, in the Willow Creek area. They usually vote alike and have developed a tradition among the families of getting their election results in first so they can have a party. Anyone who doesn't vote as the rest is thrown into Willow creek.

Cowboys vs. Indians are still in evidence in Lassen County. Bill came back to the motor home one evening with eyes as big as saucers. He had been an avid observer as a little cowboy and small Indian boy really got into a fist fight. Fists and dust were flying as they went at it when the Indian child's mother arrived on the scene, grabbed her son by the ear and led him away, scolding him. "When you get in a fight, you win!" Right on!

Our last day in Susanville was spent at the Junior Livestock Auctions preceded by an outdoor luncheon put on by the mother's of 4-H and FFA participants. I helped the ladies and also put our bags of apricots along the center of the tables. Clare purchased a lamb and we were both delighted to discover that the 4-Her who had raised it joined us for lunch and he was Bev Lane's son. Bev had been the first person we had met in Lassen County on our first trip up with Tom Sawyer in the motor home.

We were running dangerously low on gas in the vast expanse of sagebrush; we could see in all directions, there appeared like a mirage, a little gas station and beer parlor, it's cheery lights guiding us to it. While we got the motor home filled, Clare, Tom and I went in to have a beer and met Bev and the local blacksmith, who went out with us and signed the motor home. So, it was fun to meet the young carbon copy of his Dad and knew Clare's purchase had done him some good financially.

Chapter 14 Northern Counties, Alturas and Modoc

Nevada County's fair started the next day, as did Modoc's. Edwina had her work cut out arranging a schedule. In addition to the two fairs, there was an annual meeting of the Plumas-Sierra Rural Electric Cooperative to be held in Portola on Friday, a Ceres Peach Festival parade in our home town on Saturday, a parade in Cedarville, Modoc County on Sunday, plus a cattleman's barbecue in Susanville the same day. We had promised Sue Price that we wouldn't miss that one, and, Clare had promised Edwina that if she got everything properly scheduled she could go with us. We had also promised ourselves a two day vacation if we made it through this weekend. Edwina handed us the completed schedule and we were off and running, flying, hop-skip-and jumping.

We got set up at the Nevada County fair with Jeanne Dryden's expert help, the boys struck up the band, and we were settled in one of the loveliest settings of any fair in the district. The grounds are enhanced with groves of towering pines, and the paths are lined with masses of spectacularly brilliant petunias. The pines offered welcome shade in the blistering heat that we decided we were blessed with taking with us wherever we went all summer. Kim Payne stayed with the boys and Smitty to help us on our door-to-door routine. That pleased the girls, for they liked Kim and were getting tired of being bossed by their brother and Doug, the super organizer of the group.

We located our hotel, according to Edwina's instructions,

and in fifteen minutes we were in hysterics, laughing. The air conditioned rooms that she had arranged for us over the phone were cooled by two portable electric fans which created some cross-ventilation if you kept the door open between the rooms. When I tried to open the curtains, they fell in a dusty thud to the floor, and when Lynne started to hang her clothes up in the closet, the rod fell down. Oh well, we realized we were lucky to have a roof over our heads during Nevada County fair time, and we could only pray that that didn't fall down too.

The next day Max and Edwina were on hand. Max was to fly us to Frank Nervine's Beckwourth airport and Edwina to chaperon in our absence. After we left Edwina was initiated into our 'tricky closet club', and she was set for an unusual two days. That night, sitting in the front seat of the motor home at the fairgrounds while the kids did their routine, she gained an admirer in a man sporting a hard hat. The fellow wanted to buy her a beer and kept saying, with great emotion, "Lady, you are too beautiful to be a Senator's wife. You should be First Lady of the Land." As the First Lady kept graciously declining the offer, he would disappear and come back with two large cups of beer; and solemnly would toast her and then drink them both.

Meanwhile, we flew to Beckwourth, and our buddy Jack Bones picked us up and transported us to our motel on the far side of Portola. The highway was outlined with broad masses of brilliant blue from all of the wild Bachelor Buttons in full bloom.

Then we arrived at the packed Memorial Hall for the Rural Electrical Cooperative meeting. We saw that Assemblywoman Pauline Davis, whose home was in Portola, and Congressman Biz Johnson, were also there. We were especially glad that we had made the extra effort to be there. They are both well thought of in their districts and with good reason. They truly represent the people who elected them more than the average legislator. We were also pleased to note that Clare's opponent was a 'no-show' and his excuse was the fact that he had to be in Ceres the next day for the Peach Festival. Clare assured the throng that he would be in his hometown the next day, too.

When we got back to the Sleepy Pines Motel, much to our surprise, parked right next to us was Congressman Johnson's car. We seemed to bump into each other quite frequently and liked them both very much. Mrs. Johnson still remembered my Uncle Kyle from the days when he and Biz roomed together when they both were young men working for the Pacific Fruit Express. They worked California from the Imperial Valley to Roseville, where Biz subsequently launched his political career. I teased Kyle about Mrs. Johnson remembering what a good dancer he was!

The next morning we flew back to Nevada County and Edwina, Clare and Bill flew back to Modesto with Max to be in the Ceres Peach Festival Parade. 'Uncle Richard', the boys and girls and I started up the long red road to the Modoc fair in Cedarville. The warm red of the winding road through parts of northern California are forever imprinted on my memory. As we wound up through Litchfield and Standish, I got my old spooky feeling of having known this area before. I just loved these two little towns.

When we arrived in Alturas, we were tired and anxious to relax and clean up before driving over the pass to the Cedarville fair. To my dismay, and the motel owner's consternation, Dale tore up the outside stairs of the motel in four leaps, swung over the rail and dropped to the ground. Just good old animal spirits after being cooped up so long, and full of all kinds of health food drinks and vitamins, along with extra hours spent on his weight lifting equipment. Almost wild enough to get us evicted!

Clare, Bill and Max took in the Ceres Peach Festival parade which was fun, because they knew everyone along the parade route. They flew back to Nevada City in time to attend the rodeo, where Clare handed out ribbons to the winners. This time Edwina was on hand to climb under and over fences through all the manure. Thus, she discovered that it wasn't all roses that we had been experiencing these past months.

Those of us up in Modoc County piled into the motor home and headed over the craggy mountain pass from Alturas to Cedarville, a tiny town nestled at the foot of the rocky peaks and bordered by a long, narrow and shallow lake. We had a nice spot to park the Big Green Machine, and I was hurrying to fix supper when a young man stopped by, poking his head in the open door and introducing himself. He seemed like a nice kid, so I turned to introduce him to the rest of the gang, only to see the frosty, grim looks the kids were directing his way. Tom said, "Yeah, we have met him before," emphasizing the 'him' and the girls and the other boys chose to ignore him completely. He made a fast exit, and I said, "What was that all about?" Lynne piped up, "He and Debby LaCoste and another guy came by the motor home the other night, sniffed and asked if we were smoking pot, and I blew my top." It would seem that creeps come nicely packaged at times. If this punk kid was working on the LaCoste campaign I vowed to find out more about him.

We met Clare, Edwina and Max at the nearby airport the next day, and leaving the kids in Smitty's capable hands, we flew away for the Cattleman's Barbecue in Lassen County. Edwina would finally get in on the fun. The last two days had been less than fun. Two days before, as we got ready to take off for Portola, parting words to Wina had been, "You're going to love our motel – air conditioning, swimming pool, and a kitchen. It's really neat." Five minutes after she got there, she had also pulled down the curtains and the clothing rod. Then she had spotted the two little electric fans and the girls, three sweltering lumps under the covers, sound asleep.   Getting them up and determined to get them fed and their spirits revived, she ran into a stone wall called Kim Payne. Kim had been given the assignment to get the door-to-door work done, and he was determined to do so, heat or no heat. Temperatures were still over one hundred degrees, and as the heat kept up it's intensity, tempers became increasingly short. Bless Smitty who, in his calm, quiet way, got the women into the motor home and the boys headed for the business district with signs and literature. Without a word of explanation until he stopped at the top of a steep hill, got out and cheerily said, "Here's where you walk, girls," then demonstrated what he meant by shuffling in place for a few minutes. This changed the mood and everyone broke up laughing. We're not sure how much walking actually got done that day, but it's a fact that Edwina treated the girls to a great meal in an air conditioned restaurant, and it was greatly appreciated.

So, as we winged our way to the barbecue in Susanville, she had really earned one fun day. Sue Price met us at the Beckwourth airport and drove us out to the barbecue. They had a fantastic steak barbecue, and Max and Edwina nearly fell over one another getting in line, since they hadn't taken time to eat since noon the day before. All of Clare's Lassen supporters seemed to be there and we had a ball. An arena had been erected, and I watched the wives in a calf roping contest, and a team game, where one gal did the roping and her partner had to tie a ribbon on the calf's tail. Edwina and I entered a contest where you had to guess the weight of a baby buffalo, the prize being the buffalo. We guessed high, deciding that Max might object to an extra passenger. Julian Mapes wife won, thank goodness, almost hitting the exact weight. We hated to leave, but had to get back to the fair before dark, and I insisted on stopping downtown to pick up a cake for Tom's nineteenth birthday. He was very surprised and pleased that he got sort-of-a-party to honor the day.

The next day we covered Alturas door-to-door, and had done Cedarville the day before, so Max flew us up to Tulelake, the northernmost town in the district. Katherine Bailey, president of the Tulelake Basin Republican Women's Club met us, and after Clare's talk at lunch, escorted us to the newspaper publisher's office for a visit before we had to head back to Alturas. Bob Barclay, District Attorney, had a business tour lined up for Clare and a visit to the high school to meet with the students, followed by a stop at the radio station for an interview. The high school students had issues that they considered very important and wanted to know the candidates stands. The most important one was his stand on doe hunts, which he answered to their satisfaction.

We had nothing scheduled that evening, so Bill Greene, advance man for the campaign in those counties north of Kim's territory, Edwina, Clare and I decided to go out for a super dinner at a highly recommended steak house. It was nice to relax and spend a quiet evening exchanging ideas over dinner. Wina and I were laughing at how we looked, not exactly grubby, but not fashion plates, for sure, when the door opened and in streamed a large group, headed by Ernie and Jeanne LaCoste. Jeanne is a beautiful woman and she was gorgeous in a long, lacy, embroidered and slightly fantastic dress. At that moment it would have been great to be able to crawl under the table, but I bravely mustered a smile and a greeting, and was just glad that I had my back to their table. After three or four of their group came over to meet Clare, we felt better, and then from the entrance to the bar we heard persistent "Psstt Pssssstt." A finger was beckoning to Clare who was graciously ordering a bottle of wine for LaCoste's table. "Psst" came across the room once more, caught his eye attention and he got up and casually walked into the bar to see what was going on. There was impish Bob Barclay, feeling pretty tickled with himself, for he had been doing a bit of investigating and found out that some of the people in LaCoste's dinner party were not supporting him and just thought we'd like to know it.

All of us were reaching the point of exhaustion that needed the two days vacation we had scheduled. Edwina and Smitty were going to fly home with Max and find out if they still had families claiming them, and Dale had had all of the fresh air he could take for a few days and wanted to get back to Palo Alto to see his parents.

Clare had a few morning appointments so he took my car and I piled into the motor home with the kids. With Doug driving, we headed for Likely and Don and Shirley Fluornoy's cabin on the ranch. The Fluornoys and Bru Christianson were Clare's Modoc co-chairmen until Bru got tabbed by Governor Reagan to serve as Director for the California Department of Agriculture. Wes Sawyer had been instrumental in getting us together since he worked with Brumel on the State Agriculture Board. Bru Christianson and Don Fluornoy were both large built men, poster perfect for their real life roles as cattlemen and solid citizens. When Brumel and his wife Barbara left for Sacramento they were stepping out of one world and into another that would surely be a big change in their lifestyle. The Fluornoys would manage their ranch in addition to their own.

They had arranged the first breakfast meeting in Alturas when we met all of their friends and got the campaign off the ground. Now Shirley would have a busy time during haying season with all of the crews to take care of and many mouths to feed. However, she was waiting for us with a gracious welcome to their ranch and directions to the cabin. t sounded like a lot of gates. It was. Doug drove carefully down one lane after another, rut filled, and not created for the kind of vehicle we were using. Our Big Green Machine made it through one gate after another while we oohed and aahed over the beautiful valley. Green grass up to the cattle's bellies arched for miles, and wild flowers, native birds and an occasional deer and antelope caught our eye. Streams gleamed and meandered leisurely through the meadows, and we started to unwind. For sure, there wasn't a house within sight to go door-to-door. I sent up a little prayer of thanks to God for leading us to such good friends. I must admit that the captain needed a breather too, for something had come up in the last two days that had aroused everything but Christian impulses.

While we had stayed at the motel in Alturas, Lynne had received several phone calls from a young man in LaCoste's campaign. He invited her to go out with him, and kept calling after she had turned him down to the point where he was a plain nuisance. She reached the point where she recognized his voice on the phone and we would hear her say, "Oh, it's you...", and bang the receiver as she hung up. We thought very little about it at the time, but it caused Lynne to be the recipient of a bit of family teasing. t was far from a laughing matter when someone from town told us he had heard some kid talking about my daughters in an insulting way and everyone at the bar had heard him. I felt an instantaneous, murderous rage, and further investigation pointed out the culprit as the same young man on our opponent's staff that had been calling Lynne. Before we left for the cabin on Fluornoy's ranch the phones had been humming and we understood that the young man had been fired. My skin was still crawling.

Clare joined us later that afternoon, and we spent two blissful days in that heavenly spot. The cabin was made of logs, a stone fireplace, mounted animal heads on the wall in addition to a bear skin on the floor. A modern kitchen had been added for convenience. A deck on the back had built in benches and from the edge one could cast a line into the creek, bubbling over the rocks below. Trout abounded in this stream and we caught us a few. Meadows stretched north to the rocky crags which were full of caves, and it was easy to imagine Captain Jack, the leader of the Modoc Indians, living here. Shirley Fluornoy had loaned us a book about the Modoc Indians and the history of the last of the Indian wars in the United States, fought not far from here!

We quickly wound down as we strolled upstream, our eyes soaking up the view of lichen covered boulders, dancing waterfalls, and to enchant us, the soothing rush of water swirling over and around the mossy rocks. We carried our fishing poles along and fished for trout. We had a fine fish dinner and Clare spent the evening teaching the boys the fine art of rolling dice! Refreshed, and with spirits greatly renewed, we reluctantly headed for home, never being able to adequately express our gratitude for those two days.

As we traveled back south, Clare told me about his day in

Alturas before he joined us and a very interesting encounter he had with a young Indian in town. As it happened, he and the young man were both waiting to see the same man, and Clare became curious about this neatly dressed young fellow, wearing long braids and an Indian headband. He happened to be holding a LaCoste brochure in his hand which caught his eye. "I see you have one of my opponent's brochures. I'm Clare Berryhill, and I'm running for the State Senate, too." They shook hands and the young man said, "Yes, met Mr. LaCoste, but I'm not going to vote for him." Startled by such an abrupt answer, Clare asked, "May I ask why?" "He speaks with forked tongue." the Indian replied, succinctly. They chatted for a while and Clare found out that the fellow was attending college and looking for employment. When he left he was grinning. A pleasant bit of repartee and a vote for Berryhill, he hoped.

We were back in the populated area of California once again, and it was like a different world from the northern counties. Clare was the guest of Sacramento Republican Women later that week and they generously contributed money to his campaign. As Nancy Ellers, President of the club said, "We raise quite a bit of money for campaigns, Clare, and although you won't be our Senator, we want you to be elected. You are the kind of man we want in politics." Quite a morale booster. He also enjoyed an interview with Susan Sward of the Associated Press. Jack Welter's feature article about his campaign had aroused a lot of curiosity and interest in the content, and people were beginning to think that this spunky underdog just might win the election.

We always had a gang down to the ranch for the opening of dove season, but this year while the friends were still there, Sid Long took charge while we went to Amador, staying in Jackson so that Clare, Bill and Tom could hunt with Don Howard on his ranch. John Begovich, the ex-Senator, and Don's good friend would be hunting with them, so Clare could do a little 'politicking' with his dove hunting. We had first met John right after Clare had filed for the election, when the duck club Clare had been a member of for years decided to have a duck dinner prepared at a restaurant in Jackson. We were all staying the night and were having a great party when this seeming madman leaped up on our table and on over to greet one of our mutual friends. We were taking pictures at the table, and got a lulu of John, which we later sent to him, along with the negative. At a nearby table, there was another party in progress. This one was honoring the postmaster who was retiring. He was none other than Fred Cumee, chairman of the Republican Central Committee, and he was dumbfounded to discover that Clare was the Republican candidate. In the group with us was more than one Democrat face that he recognized. We met all of the people in his party and took pictures of them too, which Edwina and I delivered the following week when we were in the neighborhood. Fred became a loyal Berryhill supporter who left no stone unturned to advance the best interest of his candidate, but he certainly saw us the first time with some misgivings.

When I awoke the next morning in a motel in Amador after Clare and the boys had quietly left to go hunting out at Howard's, I realized how strange it seemed to be away from home on the opening of dove season. We had breakfast for us along with forty hunters every year, with the wives joining us for a barbecue at noon. Everyone played dominoes, napped, or told stories until the late afternoon shoot. This sleeping in was all right, but I have to admit to a little feeling of homesickness. Tom came back in and got me later, and we drove out to Howard's to a fantastic roast beef dinner, a chance to meet Don and Janice's family, and a relaxing afternoon in their lovely home.

The next two days were spent touring Tuolumne County, which brought back happy memories of our first fundraising train ride. We remembered Gil Stokes, a bit green with envy, threatening a Jesse James type hold-up, but with his reputation as a law-and-order man, he decided against it. Otis and Jean Rosasco had arranged another trip and we walked our legs off again on the round trip, since we now knew so many more of the people on the train, it was more fun. When the Tuolumne County Sheriffs Posse came whooping and hollering up to welcome the train at the Sonora depot, it was nice to know that they were being friendly. We will never forget the colorful setting at the train station, as seen from the back platform, as Berryhill boosters snaked through the crowd waving posters, with the pep band once again playing their hearts out. Then there was the posse itself, resplendent in red shirts, black hats and vests, and the whirling, stamping of their horses.

Chapter 15: The Mountains of Placer, Amador & Tuolumne Counties

We hurried home to Ceres to take the pep band on a double duty Sunday. In the morning we were in a parade in Newman, with all the arrangements handled by Gary Mall. We had a spiffy antique car to ride in and the band followed, bright eyed-and-bushy-tailed. We rushed back home and reorganized for a trip back to Tuolumne County where Dick and Marian Davey were hosting a reception at their mountain retreat in Strawberry, along the Stanislaus River.

As the motor home chugged up the hill to the Davey's cabin in Strawberry, we had a moment to gaze up the beautiful gorge of the river and think of all the fun times we had spent at our nearby cabin at Leland Creek, and of all the fishing Clare had done up and down that stretch of river. No time for nostalgia now, as we entered the Davey's cabin for the party. Many old and new friends arrived and were welcomed by the band playing down below the deck, with the sparkling, rushing water as their backdrop. We would have loved to have stayed the night with our close friends, but we had to return home for Clare to attend a Modesto Lions Club breakfast, after which he had to pick me up for a coffee klatch at the Sinclear's home in Hughson. Their son had been working hard on the campaign in Stanislaus County and it was indeed nice to be at a campaign function so close to home for a change.

I relaxed at home for a day after that while Clare left by plane for Amador County where he spent a fast-paced day in Jackson, ending with a Rotary dinner as Pat Crosby's guest. Kim took over the escorting duties in Grass Valley, with Ivan Branson, Clare's co-chairman taking him as a guest to a local meeting of the SRS club. Max picked him up once again and flew him down to Turlock where I met him and rushed, as usual, to the grand opening of the Turlock Republican headquarters opening. The building was gaily decorated and crowded with enthusiastic party faithfuls of all ages. Victory was in the air for President Nixon, and we were beginning to build our own confidence based on our recent experiences. From there, Clare had dinner with Richard Dixon, a Democrat on our side and some people from Riverbank.

We sat for half an hour late that night musing over the wide range of the days' activities, sipping a glass of wine as we unwound, and then hit the bed for a deep untroubled sleep. Refreshed and raring to go the next morning, I headed for Auburn, Placer County. This charming county seat is one of our favorite foothill towns. It is framed by railroad trestles as you approach from the west, and perches like a genuine gold nugget in the Mother Lode hills. The old town, originally the red-light district of early days, is now a successful business area, maintaining the romantic atmosphere of those early days, but bustling with shops that capture the tourists' attention. The Republican headquarters was on the south side of an island of shops, and the Democrat headquarters was situated at the other end. The ladies took a good-nature ribbing about the newly painted no-parking curbs out in front of their building, with a huge beer truck parked there. They grumbled that their real problem was the lady mayor, who happened to be a Democrat.

That evening, Clare drove down highway 80 to Rocklin where our dear friend, Jeanne Broome was having a wine and cheese tasting party on his behalf. George, Edwina and I came up in the motor home and met him there. Jeanne was laughingly telling us Clare arrived in a state of exhaustion and fell into her little girl's bed to nap before the party. Her daughter promptly put up a sign that said, "Senator Berryhill slept here!" When he arrived, the yard had not been complete, but when he arose, the nurserymen had been there and the garden had been planted. We certainly enjoyed Jeanne's first big party in her new home. Another exhausted night's sleep, back in Ceres, and we began one more day. At this point it was hard to remember yesterday or think about tomorrow, it was enough to get revved up to talk today.

Chapter 16: Amador, Calaveras, Placer County

Saturday, September ninth, Max flew Clare to Martel in Amador County to go to a Clampers shindig. I drove to my first public speaking engagement, with mouth dry, and heart pounding. Millie Reha was hosting the Republican Women's Club at her home in Pine Grove, and I was drafted to fill in for Clare. Public speaking is not my field, but as I related Clare's campaign progress, it didn't seem like a speech at all, but a friendly conversation. I discovered a lump in my throat as I explained the how and why of our involvement in this campaign, and our deep commitment to honest politics, and Republican principles. Discussing Clare's motivations and aspirations seemed totally different from 'giving a speech'. I left the peaceful forest where the Reha's lived and where I had actually enjoyed articulating our deeply held beliefs about citizen involvement in government. Clutched in my hand was a most welcome check for the campaign presented to me at the meeting.

Clare and I met later that day at Pat and Maureen Crosby's home to relax for a short while, shower and change clothes as we headed for Roseville. Gene Chappie had invited us to 'stop by' for their International Dance that night, which was to be a Mexican Fiesta under the supervision of Dave and Zeph Rodriguez. We now felt acquainted with many Roseville residents, so it was worth the long drive over to say 'hello', and also dropped in on a reception at Marty and Leroy Lyons home in Hidden Valley. Their subdivision had to be one of the most enchanting we have ever seen.

The next day was Sunday, and Uncle Richard and the kids participated in a parade without us, in Grass Valley. We had very dear friends getting married that day, and nothing would have stopped us from being with them. It was nice to touch such a beautiful part of the 'real' world for one day, for it had been a busy week. The next week sped by with Clare commuting to Calaveras County. Jimmy Oller had mapped out the town of San Andreas and Angels Camp for the girls and me to walk and gave us a welcome day's help after which was Epson Salt time for the aching feet.

Our last fair for the campaign was in Auburn from September 14th to the 17th. We felt quite lost without the pep band and the girls, but school had started and we had waved them sadly away. Doug was off to Chico State, Tom, Dennis and Lynne to Modesto Junior College, Bill and Janie to Ceres High School, and with pleasure we kept Betsy out of Fall quarter at Cal Poly, San Luis Obispo to help at home and on the campaign. It would mean a postponement of her college education, but a very special treat to have her with us. Betsy has a wonderfully uplifting attitude towards life, and as we became wearier, her bright and cheery smile would lift us up, and help keep us going. As she said, "Heck, Dad, I wouldn't be able to concentrate on school this fall anyways!"

Clare attended breakfasts, lunches and dinners in Placer County the following week and we had the family together on the weekend. We attended a gala celebration in Amador County on Saturday when a special event in honor of the Pony Express was held. We got to ride in an old stage coach through the streets of Jackson, flanked by the colorfully garbed Mountain Men astride their prancing horses. The crowd was bright with the red shirts of the many Clampers participating in the celebration.

After the parade, we drove up to Pine Grove for the dedication of a new park, and all too brief stop in Volcano, and then back to Auburn in time for Gino Chappie and Clare to hop into a helicopter at the fairgrounds for a flight to Kirkwood Means to attend the opening of the newly refinished highway 88.

It was the end of an interesting week in Placer County, getting to meet Joe Varni and visiting his farm to see his prize ponies, the 4-H barns at the Junior Livestock Auction, and a most pleasant afternoon with Dave Hughes, touring Forest Hill, a small lumber town high on a ridge above Auburn and the American River. Dave had been talked into serving as our escort by his wife, an active Republican Club member. We felt like we were old friends by the time the afternoon had passed, for it turned out that one of Dave's hobbies was horse racing, and since we were the proud owners of a thoroughbred mare, and looking forward to racing her colt, we talked blood lines and horses for several hours.

On Saturday night we stayed in Jackson after attending the annual Calaveras Committee barbecue at the Frog-town fairgrounds just out of Angels Camp. Pinky and Ike Moore met us with open arms. Ike was holding a butcher knife, not for us, but he was head chef, as usual, and in the midst of preparing one of his famous meals. Congressman Bob Mathias was present as he was in a tough campaign of his own in the newly re-apportioned Congressional District. A band replete with 'gut-bucket' and assorted unusual instruments played for dancing, and it turned out that they were from close to our hometown, having traveled from Hilmar to entertain.

We had a few days for me to stay home and help Betsy get organized to run the old homestead, and then Clare and I took off for South Lake Tahoe to meet local business people, to North Lake Tahoe for a Republican function, and on up to Sierra County for a dinner that Russ Turner had invited us to. The adventure meant a lot of driving before arriving home on Friday. The dinner in Loyalton, Sierra County, introduced me to one of the biggest characters I'd ever met. A big man in his fifties, he arrived late, and had obviously just gotten off the tractor. He had a resonant voice, which seemed to please him more than anyone else. Full of the drama of his life, he regaled me with stories of his remarkable recovery from a nearly fatal heart attack, his many meetings over the years with Governor Reagan and numerous sundry of other celebrities. By the time dessert arrived, my head was swimming. He really seemed larger than life, and I had an unusually good time visiting with him.

We were home Friday and looking forward to our trip to Penryn the following day with Esther and Bill Noda along with Kiyo and Naomi Yamamoto, who were going up with us in the motor home to take in the annual Buddhist Festival. The rest of the family followed us up in the car so they could return home while we continued on the campaign trail. It was really amusing to hear a lady ask Naomi the symbolic meaning of the many intricate and ornate items decorating the temple. Looking helpless and equally puzzled, Naomi replied, "I don't know. I'm Presbyterian." We all left, full of delicious food we had purchased at the many booths, and arms loaded with Bonsai trees we were hopefully taking home to raise. Esther had told us of her family taking their family bonsais with them to the relocation centers during the war, as one of their most prized possessions.

Tom, Lynne, Betsy and Janie were dropped of at good old Johnson Hall in Roseville to participate in a door-to-door walk with the local Young Republicans. They were very impressed with a handout one of the boys, a Mexican-American, had done in Spanish to be handed out that day, also. With help like that how could their Dad lose?

Billy, Clare and I drove back to Stanislaus County and on over to Hickman where the Warner's have their ranch along the banks of the Tuolumne River. They were hosting a Farm Folks for Berryhill Potluck dinner, complete with prizes, and all for the price of one dollar. We sure didn't want to miss that, for it had come about in such a nice way. The first inkling we heard that the dinner was even going to be held was when a lady came up to Edwina at the booth at the Stanislaus County Fair, and asked if she could leave some tickets for the dinner to be sold at the booth. Edwina was a little suspicious, for any other events usually had her up to her eyes working, planning, and selling tickets. This group had decided, on their own, to have this evening fundraiser for Clare and didn't want to bother him when he was so busy. They all knew him and didn't care whether he was there or not, they just wanted to raise a little money. They sold 200 tickets and the prizes were quite an assortment, from a sack of onions to a butchered steer, and many things in between. The picnic grounds on their property along the river bank was packed with our old friends from the battle over the Tuolumne River days and we had one fine time, eating and socializing. Wes Sawyer was in a fine position as a most informed Master of Ceremonies, and just before we left he quieted everyone down and pointed to the full moon that was just coming up behind us. Clear as a bell there was a cloud formation lit up in the shape of a huge V with the moon centered in it. He asked if we all didn't think that was a fine omen for the evening, and for the final victory? You bet we did! We went home with happy hearts.

Sunday morning found us dashing about Stanislaus County, managing to take in a Kiwanis breakfast first, then over to Oakdale to take in part of the annual rodeo, and then ending up in Patterson with Mimi Draper. She brought us up to date with tales of her campaigning and introduced us to Peter Lopez, an artistically talented young man. The groups that Mimi had gathered together to meet and talk to Clare were kids from Mexican backgrounds, and it was refreshing to listen to them discuss their outlook on school, politics, and local problems. Peter and Clare made a date for lunch to another meeting in Patterson with some college and high school students that couldn't be there that Sunday. We munched on the delicious giant Mexican cookies that one of the girls' mother had baked, hot, sweet, and delicious.

The following week was spent by Clare attending Chamber of Commerce and civic luncheons, working with the people from Fred Wade's public relations firm, taking in a Modesto Youth Rally organized by Dottie Spellman for the Republican Women's Club, and a trek to Meadow Mont, up in the mountains in Calaveras county. We took some of our supporters from Stanislaus County along in the motor home to join us at the meet-the-candidate dinner. We attended the Stanislaus County annual Easter Seals Dinner, Clare's favorite charity. The next night, Friday, Phil Paul had a big bash planned in Turlock. He and Georgia had worked like Trojans to host a fundraising dinner for Clare in the Assyrian Hall. Bob Mathias was there to introduce Clare, and the room was packed with well-wishers. When Phil does something, he does it well, and we were overwhelmed with the evening.

Bright and early the next morning we met with a large contingent of youngsters who were eager to go door-to-door in Modesto for Clare. Penny and Esther helped get them going and then we met back at Graceada Park at noon for hot dogs and back to the sidewalks once again for a full day of walking. Later in the evening we relaxed and enjoyed the cuisine at the annual Greek Festival. It is not the Army alone that travels on it's stomach, for this could well be a guide for 'Eating Your Way Through a Campaign'. We did it again when we went back to Patterson, taking Kathy Vaughn with us to talk to the Mexican-American youngsters in Patterson, and once again eating the giant Mexican cookies. We were full and tired.

One of the first outward indications that Clare was being looked upon as a possible winner occurred in Patterson a few days later. Mimi and Brice Draper were going through the downtown with us, and as I glanced across the circle drive in the center of town, I noticed two men getting out of a car and thought they looked familiar. "Mimi," I queried, "who are those two fellows?" "Darned if I know," she replied. "Out-of-towners, I think. Wonder what they are doing here?" This gives you an idea how small towns operate. One strange car in town sets off speculation. We moseyed over to meet our husbands, still keeping an eye on the strangers. As we drew nearer I recognized the two men as being from Sacramento, and something in my mind went 'click'. They were scouting Clare and that had to be good news. Clare came up and greeted them with surprise and we went over to the hotel to quench our thirst and visit. It was good news. They had toured the entire district, and to them, Clare looked like a real winner. Jim Chipponeri could have told them that and saved them the trouble, for he was doing a little scouting of his own and he delivered hay in far and hear parts of the district. It was early October and we were beginning to feel pretty good about the election.

On the 4th of October, Dick Davey was putting on a spaghetti feed in Ceres to raise money and give Clare a chance to visit with the old hometown. Clare's old friend, Jake Dillon, was the master chef and early in the morning, as Marian Davey and I set up and decorated tables in the community center, the odor of his pots of famous spaghetti sauce assailed out nostrils with pleasure and anticipation. We hoped a lot of people would come, and advance ticket sales had been great, so the day seemed to promise a good time. Did they come! Clare stood for close to four hours, greeting and chatting with old friends. The rest of us pitched in to help in the kitchen and that was hectic! Jake's, his son Jackie, Marian and Dick, Dorothy and Wayne Johnson, Sid and Linda Long and Ken and Betty Buoy in addition to our assorted children, worked like mad trying to keep ahead of the dishes, the salad, the spaghetti, and all those DISHES. Betty Buoy tore over to her mother's house for more dish towels and someone else ran to the store to get more spaghetti, since we ran out. The tantalizing odor of hot garlic bread kept us hungry and frustrated, with no time to eat. When Jake puts on a spaghetti feed, it is really something to see. We all went to bed completely done in, but also wonderfully content and proud of our hometown friends.

Chapter 17: Calaveras, Amador and Stanislaus County

Clare left at six in the morning the next day to fly to Auburn where Gene Chappie met him and took him to Colfax for breakfast with the mayor and city councilmen. At one-thirty he was back in Modesto for a Chamber of Commerce visit with Bill Hammond, lunch at the Sportsmen of Stanislaus Club, and afternoon meetings with his staff. he next day was Friday and we wound up the week with the annual United Crusade Dinner at the Modesto Elks Club. Jack Veneman was the main speaker, then an undersecretary of Health, Education and Welfare to the Nixon administration. He was certainly his old gracious self, but I was still stinging from his treatment of Clare in the first campaign. That grudge would take a long time to go away.

Saturday we had the glorious and rare treat to be able to sleep in, and wouldn't you know, eyes wide awake at six o'clock, and the old wheels spinning. We loafed around the ranch all day and then attended a beautiful wedding in the evening. It seemed like the only way we could squeeze in a day off was to have some close friends get married. At least the campaign was fostering romance and we didn't know of any divorces because of it!

Sunday we drove once again up to Pat and Maureen Crosby's house in Sutter Creek, where Clare had a chance to give an interview to a free-lance reporter, Mike Dunn. No matter how hard he had tried to get an opportunity to speak with the lumber workers, the union had successfully blocked his path. They had endorsed Clare's opponent and the workers simply never had a chance to hear the other candidate. We hoped that with his interview, his thoughts might come across to the public, and we had found also, that the mountain grapevine was giving him some credibility with the people. They were becoming sympathetic towards him either in spite of, or because of, the adamant union leaders. Mountain people don't like to be dictated to by anyone. Mike and Clare had a good visit, and we kept our fingers crossed that some good would come out of their encounter.

That afternoon we attended a Young Republican barbecue at the Elks Club. They were holding it to welcome Gene Chappie and his motorcade, which were making a swing throughout the district to bolster the troops. It was confusing to see people out of context in the campaign, for many who were part of Gene's group were from Roseville, and I had to mentally sort people, county by county.

During the evening hours we attended a reception at Don and Janice Howard's home so Clare could meet another group of people. It was a lovely party in their comfortable ranch style home. The house was built of adobe bricks, with large beamed ceilings, a roaring fire in the fireplace, and comfortable people to be with too. Their special guest was John Begovich, and his presence gave a clue to his sentiments with all of the Democrats who were there, without him having to give a formal endorsement. We were charged up for the drive home and it was remarkable how little we even thought about the distances we were driving almost daily.

Don Schneider of radio station KTRB in Modesto, took off a day to fly Clare to Quincy to tour the Feather River College, attend a Rotary luncheon, tour the Crescent Lumber Mill, and then fly back home for an evening reception at Phil and Georgia Paul's new home in Turlock. They had a packed house and we found ourselves surprised to find large groups of people in Turlock that we had never met. In this case, the new acquaintances were mostly from the State College in Turlock, a relatively new campus. Clare had friends there, however, for they were all aware that they wouldn't have gotten their new science building if Clare, then Assemblyman, hadn't worked to get it into the budget. He and Senator Teale, who was on the budget conference committee, had worked in conjunction to convince Governor Reagan that this was a worthwhile project. The Governor cooperated with Clare at all times, and Clare appreciated the fact that he did. Georgia had tables laden with dish after dish of tantalizing Assyrian dishes, the torches lining the yard gave off a warm glow, and we all had a great evening in their lovely new home.

In the morning we drove to Sonora, where Kim met us and took us on another tour of the business district along with a candidates night at the American Legion Hall. We returned home that night, really very weary.

The next evening there was a scheduled Chamber of Commerce meeting with the candidates in the small, rural community of Denair. I was quite excited, for it was to be held in the new multi-purpose room of the elementary school where I had taught when we were first married. Memories rushed back to me, and I looked forward to seeing a lot of people from the town that I seldom had a chance to see. It would also give us a chance to see how Ernie and Jeanne were doing, for our paths didn't cross very often these days. The pace was getting so high pitched that we scarcely knew what the opposition was doing. He had the Modesto Bee giving his proposed legislation a great many headlines, but Clare's earlier maneuver to put the 'kibosh' on questionable advertising was successful. The tone of Ernie's ads were much less flamboyant than the last time. He did have a number of bills that he was pushing hard, but little of substance had actually been passed and signed into law. What little we heard from the hills indicated that he was walking the business districts with little or no impact. There really wasn't time to worry about him.

If my memory had been functioning better, I might have known that Wednesday night in Denair is the wrong night of the week to schedule a public gathering. This is church night, and sure enough, the only people there were the LaCostes, the Berryhills, Edwina, Lee Madsen, the Chamber of Commerce contact, and the man who was to provide coffee for the people. We decided to relax, chat a bit and all went home early. That was the only time that had happened.

Bright and early the next morning Betsy and I were in the large audience for the annual Good Egg Breakfast at the SOS club in Modesto. Governor Reagan was to be honored as the Good Egg of the year, and we never missed a chance to see and hear this fine man express his courage, convictions and common sense. There were so many people there by 7 a.m. that we barely got seats. Clare had to rush after the breakfast to make other commitments in Modesto and Turlock, where I joined him in the evening for a Lions Club Ladies night. Flo and Cal Weese were there and we tried to catch up on the news, while Clare joked around with the club members. He had been President of the Ceres Lions and had bowled against these fellows for a long time, so the evening didn't seem like camping. It felt more like old home week, although we did nothing that wasn't geared to the upcoming election.

On Friday, the thirteenth of October, I set out with trepidation for San Andreas to fill in for Clare at the grand opening of their headquarters. Betsy accompanied me for moral support, and since her friend Jimmy Oller would be there, it would be fun for her. As usual, the stage fright was unwarranted, for when we arrived at the building situated on the steep main street of the town, it was a crowd of people I was well acquainted with, and they were having a good time. The cable television interview went fine, too, perhaps because of the champagne that was served at the open house.

At any rate, both Betsy and I had fun, and left reluctantly for Ceres, and an evening with the Stanislaus Central Committee along with the Republican Women who were hosting a celebrity champagne party to raise funds for Candidates. Clare's staff had spent many hours trying to line up celebrities for them, starting out with the idea of corralling the 'Duke' himself, John Wayne. When that didn't jell, we went through the list of entertainers who often made themselves available for such Republican events. Talk about feeling humble. No one could make it from the glittering world of Hollywood, so Bev Zaumeyer and Vick Hollis took Berryhill bumper stickers and pasted names of various Republican celebrities on them. As everyone came in we stuck a bumper sticker on their back and then they had to guess who they were. It got pretty hilarious when we sneaked in Pat Paulsen for President on one man, and in all the around I almost missed seeing who I was slapping a bumper sticker on - State Controller Hugh Fluornoy. "Oops," I gulped. "You're a real celebrity," as I slapped a goofy name on his back. Friday the 13th turned out to be a really neat day.

Chapter 18: Stanislaus and El Dorado County

Saturday dawned overcast and threatening as we set out with the band for one more parade, this time in Waterford. By the time we got the band lined up, the truck all decorated and were ready to start the parade route, it started to pour. Edwina and I looked like two drowned rats, and wouldn't you know, the opponent's wife looked like a million bucks – as usual. Oh well, we were in a friendly territory and were enthusiastically greeted by the local people who lined the street, rain or no rain.

I fervently prayed that the good old electric curlers would last out the campaign, as Edwina and I curled our hair all of the way to Roseville that evening while Clare and George sat at the front of the motor home. We had told them about so many of the parties at Johnson Hall, and this was their only chance to see, first hand. Edwina was a bit behind the rest of us for the Sons of Italy dinner, because she was still drying her hair out in the motor home. The evening was just great, so it had been worth it. We were four very weary campaigners when we got home that night. Clare had a welcome Sunday off, to catch his breath.

Monday, the sixteenth of October, Clare spent in Turlock, touring business with Jim Bainbridge and Jim Lindsey, attending the Lions Club with Will Keener and then spending the afternoon at Stanislaus State College. The college Democrat Club had invited their candidate to speak, so Patty Hollingsworth, who was on the college staff in charge of student activities, called on Clare to appear also. He looked forward to the confrontation very much, since he felt confident talking to students even if they disagreed with him. He always made friends while thoroughly enjoying the give and take in these situations. To Clare's surprise and the great delight of Patty, Ernie was a 'no show'. The Young Democrats had put out lots of publicity and had quite a crowd gathered to hear their candidate. Whatever the reason for not putting in an appearance, the bad manners of not letting them know he wasn't going to be there was most unfortunate for him and a great opportunity for Clare. Betsy accompanied her Dad and was enjoying being in her element on the college campus. They spent as much time as the students wanted, discussing issues and philosophy. Clare and Betsy came home totally wound up and talking a mile a minute.

My day had been eventful too, since I had driven to Auburn to fill in again, with a chance to speak to the Auburn Soroptomist Club. Doris Walker had met me and we visited the headquarters in Old Town, dropped in to see the little shops I never had time to visit when I was trying to keep up with Clare, and then went up to the hotel for the luncheon. I had a lovely time and enjoyed sharing our experiences in the campaign with this informed and friendly group of women.

Tuesday the Methodist Church in Turlock conducted a 'Legislative Workshop' in conjunction with the League of Women Voters panel discussion of the propositions that would appear on the ballot. All of the candidates had agreed to be there to speak, except Clare, who had a previous commitment. Therefore, I filled in again, with nerves jangling over being in the same program with our opponent. No one could say many derogatory things about my husband without raising my ire and I could feel my whole body begin to shake. Listening to him 'blow his own horn' and speaking patronizingly about his opponent did nothing to alleviate the shakes. It was with great effort that I tried and hopefully drummed up a smile when it was my turn to speak. Self control prevailed and I stuck to the simple statement I knew so well, refusing to be goaded into lowering the standard of ethics we had set for the campaign. It was most difficult, but as Grandma used to caution me, "You get more flies with honey than vinegar."

We spent one day touring in nearby Oakdale and then drove to Tahoe for two fully scheduled days. Ralph Anderson held a 'coffee' in his home overlooking the changing patterns of blue in the lake and the blue peaks of the Sierra bordering it. Clare mingled with the Tahoe residents. They discussed their deep concerns about regional government., TRPA and CTRPA, the Tahoe basin development and other problems unique to the areas. It seemed unfortunate that the Tahoe area is divided geographically north and south by Placer and El Dorado Counties. The problems of the west side of the mountains are so different from the lake side. Solutions are complicated by two sets of county supervisors, the regional agencies and mountain range. It certainly is a beautiful place in which to campaign, and I blithely tagged along, enjoying Clare's talks at coffee klatches, an interview on Cable vision, a huge cocktail party at Felice and Bill Johnson's home, again. After the party at the Supervisor's home, the men went on to the Rotary Club dinner where Clare gave a low-key talk, and the ladies took me out to dinner, culminating a full day.

We stayed the night at our friends, the Cavalier's motel and started at first light the next morning with John Reitz and his son, touring businesses, and then he took us to South Lake Tahoe High School. Will Clugg, on the faculty, had set up a classroom for a question and answer session, which was Clare's best mode of campaigning. Will was the chairman of the El Dorado Central Committee, so he enjoyed the repartee as much as we did. When our time was up on campus, we hurried to meet Henry Butler. Henry had put together a group of people to have lunch with us at Poor Pierre's. Henry first came to Lake Tahoe when the only means of transportation to this area was by train. His home on the edge of the lake is an oasis in an otherwise commercialized area. Wandering the paths in his corner of the forest was like being a million miles from the hubbub of the '70's. We would have gladly spent the rest of the day listening to Mr. Butler spin talks about the Lake Tahoe he had known for so long, but duty called and we reluctantly hit the campaign trail again.

Tommy Stewart, another Supervisor, hosted a most pleasurable coffee party at this home on the Tahoe Keyes. We had just enough time to rush back to the motel to change for a major fundraiser being held that evening at the Edgewood Country Club. Senator Fred Marler and his wife, Irene, drove up to speak on Clare's behalf before a large and jovial crowd. Our good Dr. DenDulk came all of the way from home to join us, as he always did – perhaps Clare's most loyal supporter.

The next day, Friday the 20th, we headed back down the hill to the western slope of El Dorado County for a day's tour. Maria Nicholas from Carmel was going to tape some TV of the campaign, so we were quite excited. We first met in Pollock Pines, winding our way through the peaceful forest lane to Pete Hansen's home for coffee and a chance to meet the neighborhood. Pete is a retired navy commander and we had to envy him and his wife for their blissfully relaxed lifestyle. The cameras filmed the group and then we headed for the Michigan-Cal Lumber Company in Camino for some more footage. Maria found that she had to hurry in order to meet Clare's opponent and do his half of the interview.

We toured Apple Hill, which was in the middle of their annual Apple Hill Festival. At harvest time the local farmers join together to sell their apple crop, and with the publicity from their well organized festival, they do a roaring business. A beautiful drive on a fall day, the Hill winds among apple orchards and Christmas tree farms. Stands are set up at each farm to sell apple cider and baked goods. Dick Moss, Clare's chairman, was driving us and as we wound around the twisting roads, he got angrier and angrier. He and his twin boys had done a thorough job putting up Berryhill signs on ranches with the owner's permission. The night before they had all been torn down and LaCoste's put up. Angry apple growers were out tearing them down. We arrived at the main center of festival activities, where all sorts of apple deserts are served, and there is an arts and crafts exhibit, also. Our adrenaline was running high after the political sign affair, so we sat and had an apple dessert while Dick Moss cooled down enough for us to go over and say "hello" to the opponent. Maria felt this was a great coincidence, so she could get an interview with both candidates at the same time. Naturally, Jeanne and I both said that OUR husband was going to win, but I got in the last word.

That night we attended the gala annual Chappie Oktoberfest in Placerville, with a large crowd of supporters of Gene's from both parties. Clare had an opportunity to meet the people in an informal atmosphere, and it was a fun evening. We heard from a Democrat in the crowd that LaCoste was appearing across town at a Democrat rally, accompanied by Assemblyman John Burton, the city legislator in Placerville. One of Gene's Democrat friends drove over to see what was going on, and came back to report that there were very few people there, with most everyone at Gene's party. We got to meet some of those who attended the LaCoste function later in the evening when we went over to Skip Miller's house. A group of teachers were there and they wanted the candidates to listen to them. Listen we did until 2 a.m., but felt that it had been worthwhile. Clare and the teachers present had several honest differences of opinion. It was a loudly stimulating discussion on the subject of their school problems.

We stayed overnight at the friendly Mother Lode Motel where we had stayed during the fair, and the next day went to a 'coffee' at Ginny and Dick Burlington's home. They had a warm, homey house filled with antiques that they had lovingly and painstakingly refinished. From Bullington's house, situated above Placerville in the pines, we drove down to Diamond Heights for another 'coffee' at the Grimes home. We then had lunch with Vernon and Delores Garcia, Dolores serving as Clare's treasurer in the county. They had invited a forest ranger over to chat with Clare over sandwiches, and they had time for a deep discussion over fire fighting practices and other topics.

After a restful afternoon at the Garcia's, we drove down Highway 50 to Anita and Harold Boel's home in El Dorado Hills, where Anita and her friend, Pat Lacy had a wine tasting party to introduce Clare to their neighbors. We found out later that Anita had bet Bill Ketchum $40.00 that LaCoste would win. She figured she couldn't lose entirely. Anita is a Republican, but thought a one-time loser couldn't beat an incumbent. We would have loved to have spent more time visiting with them, but needed to catch a few minutes rest before the big evening ahead.

The fundraiser that evening was to be held at Lieutenant Governor Ed Reinecke's ranch, perched high on a ridge behind Placerville. What a beautiful and peaceful spot Ed and Jean Reinecke have. Driving up the winding dirt road to the house there was a herd of Charolais cattle grazing. They looked as though they had been scrubbed and placed there to serve as a decoration, like a bouquet of flowers on a dinner party table. White painted fences sparkled in the late afternoon sun, and the hills behind their home, lower in the valley, glowed in the rosy cast of the lowering sun.

We had been so busy for the past three days that we hadn't even had time to savor the anticipation of this evening. Lucky for us lots of people had been working full time to put on the greatest fund raiser we ever hope to attend. The Placerville Y.R.'s were busily parking cars, and we were simply astonished when we saw the size of the crowd. Ed and Jean's place was packed. There were supporters from all over the district, there to enjoy the hospitality, the fantastic pit-barbecued beef, and the camaraderie, as well as to give Clare a rousing welcome. People we had grown to love from all over the district had the opportunity to meet each other for the first time and compare campaign stories. The whole evening was so perfect that it was like a dream, but Ed had his realities to face. The picture I will carry with me always, is the one of our handsome Lieutenant Governor, Stetson pushed back off his forehead, rushing back and forth with wrenches, fuses, a worried look, trying to cope with the mechanical problems that went with a party of this size at his house. Jane Hamilton and the gals from the local Republican Women's Club had done a magnificent job, organizing and selling tickets throughout the district, and it seemed like everyone we knew or had ever known was on hand. No matter what life brought us in the future, we would always have the memory of a picture perfect night, with the moon amid the stars looking near enough to touch in that clear air. We made a lot of memories and a lot of money.

Chapter 19: Stanislaus and Tuolumne County

It was a temptation to bask in the memory of that wonderful evening, but the race was still on and we had to force ourselves to get up the momentum again. Clare was busy in Stanislaus County, tying up loose ends, and Edwina agreed to go with me for a two day jaunt up to the hills. First we attended a Republican Club luncheon in Angels Camp where I had a brief talk with Clare's supporters. We then drove the winding road to West Point to deliver some signs to another supporter. The day was far from over, however, since we had an evening engagement at Bear Valley Lodge at 6 o'clock. It was just a shame that Clare and Betsy had a firm commitment at a Stanislaus State function that evening, for they would have loved the evening we got to spend with the group. Betty Cooper and her brother, Bruce Orvis, who have the lodge and the resort development, were rightfully proud of their project. The main part of the lodge is a huge, sunken lounge framed at one end with a magnificent rock fireplace, and on the sides by huge decorative banners hanging from the ceiling. In front of the roaring fire they had set up a table laden with snacks and wine, with local people chatting amiably as we came downstairs. We certainly enjoyed the evening, meeting many young residents of Bear Valley, many who worked there. We were surprised to see Jim Chipponeri's daughter Cindy and her husband, who were working at the lodge and the ski hill. Issues were freely discussed with this articulate group of young voters, and I was certainly grateful that Assemblyman Chappie was also there. He handled the issues and Edwina and I became better acquainted with the people. It was an elegantly informal party, and we certainly appreciated the effort these supporters had made on Clare's behalf. The next morning at breakfast we visited with some of the young people again, and reluctantly headed back to the 'flatlands'.

Clare had the unhappy task of serving as a pallbearer for his long time friend and neighbor, Frank Neiberger. He and his wife, Gitta had taken an interest in Clare since he had been a little tyke, and had sold him their property when they decided to retire. They were hard working German immigrants, who had no family of their own. They took a real interest in their neighbor's families. It was a sad occasion for Clare, but something he had to do.

Betsy and I headed for Roseville to participate in a novel fundraiser that Clare's friend had dreamed up. They were having an out-of-the-ordinary bake sale. When we arrived, we were overwhelmed at the number of cakes and the creativity expressed in decorating them. There was an elephant cake, a mountain greenery scenery cake replete with miniature Berryhill signs and dozens of others, each unique. One of the men conducted an auction not only for the crowd that was present, but also by Ma-Bell's resources, thus widening the fun and participation. Betsy made instant friends with a darling AFS student from Germany, and they talked ninety miles an hour the whole evening. She was getting a good taste of grassroots politics in America. It was late when we got home, but the kinks from driving at night were worth the evening we had enjoyed.

The end of the week was another highlight of the campaign, as Otis and Jean Rosasco and John Lowe had organized another train trip. This time it had been arranged to accommodate more residents from Stanislaus County by starting down in Jamestown, traveling down to Oakdale where those of us from below boarded. Clare got on in Tuolumne, and the train chugged and tooted for a hilarious ride down, up, and down again. The old steam engine was just grand, and everyone loved seeing the elegant barber shop on board, the outdoor seats, and the music filled club car. Going strong under the gently swaying tiffany lamps was a banjo, a honky-tonk piano and singer, plus John Lowe's daughter and friend wandering up and down the aisles with a guitar. Everyone relished the buffet catered once again by Jack Eddy from Twain Harte Lodge.

Chapter 20 Seeing is Believing

Betsy and Tom took off one day the following week on a special assignment. Clare thought that since he had a conflict in his schedule, that they would be perfect to represent him at Sierra College in Rocklin, Placer County. They had a fine grasp of the issues, certainly had immense pride in their Dad, and we were sure they would have no problems. They not only had no problems, they turned out to be a great team for the campaign.

Clare had a television tape and live appearances to do at this time, so Kim Payne was assigned the task of appearing on his behalf at Davis High School in Modesto. Betsy and I sneaked into the audience to see the show. Representing LaCoste was Barry Wyatt, his Administrative Assistant. It infuriated me every time I saw him campaigning for his boss when his salary was paid by the state, and he had a job to do, that of running the district office. Kim carried the day beautifully with his classic, sympathy provoking "WOW" when asked touchy questions, such as, "How does Berryhill stand on lowering the drinking age to eighteen?" Very carefully Kim would explain Clare's stand to initial groans from the audience. By the time he would finish by saying "Mr. Berryhill doesn't want one single accident on his conscience, after all, he has five kids of his own." Some of the students would be nodding in agreement, or muttering under their breath, "He sounds just like my Dad!" We were proud of Kim and felt that he came off better than smoothie Barry, but then we were prejudiced.

Clare was spending some time in Placer County and coincident to his schedule, the Placer County Central Committee and Republican Women's club were putting on a fundraising dinner for him. The very special guest speaker was none other than Governor Ronald Reagan, and he had also invited Allen Grant, President of the California Farm Bureau to sit at the head table. The dinner committee had sold out well in advance, not only in their immediate area, but a bus load was coming up to Auburn from Stanislaus County. Betsy and I rode up on the bus, with all the hometown folks which included my aunts, uncles and Clare's mother and family. We were especially anxious for them to see how the campaign was really going, for they got very nervous sitting at home reading the Modesto Bee, finding out all about Clare's opponent and not enough about their boy. We felt that only by getting them up in the hills could they see and feel the enthusiasm that gave us such a feeling of confidence. 'Seeing is believe', as the saying goes. Everyone had a good time on the bus trip to Auburn, and it was a thrill to see the packed hall full of well-wishers.

The Governor was in fine fettle and his humor and support for Clare's candidacy roused everyone to a fever pitch of excitement. The family caught the spirit, and I don't think they worried half as much after that evening. Allen Grant had a few kind words to say about the way Agriculture in California needed this kind of man in Sacramento, and his presence was also appreciated. The Governor's constant backing was something we will never forget, and the man remained a good friend to Agriculture along with Clare the entire time he was in office. With just six days to go until election day, the evening was a fitting climax to eight months of campaigning. Allen Grant was criticized by LaCoste, but Allen just smiled benignly and said "I'll be happy to speak at a fundraiser for Mr. LaCoste, if the Governor asks me!"

This election time we were prepared for last minute 'dirty tricks' and Clare had taken some precautions to avoid any false advertising about him. In 1970 we were caught off guard with no time to respond to misleading newspaper ads. This year Ray and Clare had sent copies of the previous untrue, or at least mar-

SPECIAL.....AND THEN SOME

ginally true, but highly unethical ads to every paper and radio station, including the office Assembly Records which proved Clare's record, and which proved that LaCoste statements were off base. Sure enough, an ad was submitted to one of the outlets in the far north where our opponent thought we probably wouldn't know about it. Instead, the publisher checked the story and consequently refused to print it. Don't get mad, get even, as our friend Chappie always said. Clare had established control over this potential problem for the remaining few days until the election, quite a relief when we thought back to the situation the time before.

No matter what the outcome of the election, we knew that each of us involved in the campaign, and especially Clare, had done absolutely everything possible to win with honesty and integrity. Looking back on the primary race we realized that it had been a blessing in disguise, for it forced the issues early and created the opportunity for Clare to get out and meet the folks while his eventual opponent was still tied up in Sacramento. We had fine local people heading up the campaign in each community, and after school was out and the primary behind us, we accomplished our goal of having young people involved. They contributed mightily to the overall effect. Clare had become a very special candidate and the voters had responded enthusiastically to him. Everyone had done their job to the best of their ability. Our billboards reflected a fresh approach to politics, the television advertising was held to a minimum, and, we had worked our tails off.

The last weekend before the election we had a Car Caravan through the Mother Lode Trail, starting in Roseville. We met at a shopping center, attached balloons and signs to all of the cars, vans, and the Big Green machine. An unforgettable memory is that of Dennis Barbour from Ceres, long platinum hair flying, wearing a hippy hat, with two dozen balloons adorning his van, tooting, waving, and stopping to give little children some balloons as he drove through Lincoln. He certainly didn't look like your typical conservative young Republican in the least. Two days didn't allow enough time to hit our beloved northernmost counties, but we would have fun covering what we could. We will never forget looking back at the cars and friends winding up the hill behind us in Auburn, where a fine mist was falling, giving the hills and trees the aspect of a Japanese landscape. A hazy glow was cast by the fall foliage and there was a moment of an eerie feeling of unreality to find ourselves there. Dr. Den-Dulk was having a grand time in the caravan, and Edwina was in her element in the motor home, playing hostess. She had finally talked Dennis Barbour out of his hippy hat and the brim kept flopping over her smiling face.

That night we stayed at Rainbow lodge up near Donner Summit on Highway 80. An old resort of great charm, it was owned by George Ground's cousin and another fellow. They made us feel right at home. Edwina was in her element playing waitress and making everyone comfortable. Clare was relaxed and having a ball with all of his friends, and the evening came to a perfect finish when a light snow fell, turning the hills into pristine white beauty. Phil Paul was like a little kid out playing in the snow with Georgia and some of the gang having snow ball fights. The next morning, Ester and Bill Noda were out bright and early for a hike in the snow. Rainbow Lodge said they always ordered a little snowstorm for campaign caravans.

We headed up the old 49er trail and were met by Dick Moss and the Placerville bunch at Cool, home of Gene Chappie. With our enlarged entourage we wound through El Dorado County, honking and waving. We continued on down the trail to Amador where we were joined by their troops at the park on the main street for a picnic. What a fun day that was! At the conclusion of the picnic Sunday afternoon, everyone tiredly started for home. Many heads were shaking at the size of the district, comprehending what Clare had been going through somewhat better. They really had seen only a section of it, for the northern counties would have taken at least two more days. I think we succeeded in helping our friends realize that we didn't love 'home' less, but rather, like each additional child that comes to a family, there is always more love to go around. That's how we felt about the mountain counties.

Tuesday morning found us excitedly setting off with our three proud new voters, Betsy, Tom and Lynne, to cast our ballets at Yori's Grove, down the road from the ranch. We were warmly greeted by our friends and neighbors who were working on the election board, and we all grinned at the kids as they finished exercising their newly acquired privilege of voting. We knew we had five votes, at least.

Clare and his buddies were once again heading for the golf course, and I had made up my mind that this time I was going to do what I felt best doing on election day – walking precincts. As I sorted out my thoughts and emotions that morning, it came to mind that over the years, politics had been our main shared hobby. The family life we shared and the daily lifestyle we enjoyed had always been very close. By helping on election day as hard as I could, it would be rather like putting the finishing touches on this period of our life. Assuming that Clare would win, nothing would ever be quite the same again, and it was with mixed emotions that I let myself think to the future for a moment. This time we would move and thus give Clare a needed refuge from the capitol and also give us a chance to maintain our family continuity. It was a toss up as to who would be more affected by change, but we were all determined to hang on to the remembrance that each of our moves was guided by a Higher Principle. We would continue to rely on Principle to take us through each new day. As long as we worked together, and it was right, it would work.

Bev Zaumeyer was startled when I called to ask to be put to work. As it happened, the precinct just south of us wasn't covered, so we went to work to get the job done. I had worked those precincts for twenty years and had nothing less than a joyful heart as we systematically began our job.

We had all of the staff out to the ranch the night before for a barbecue. All the gang was there. Uncle Richard and his family, Rae and Mary Codoni, Edwina and George Ground, Bev and Roger Zaumeyer, Kim Payne, Esther Morrison, and the teenagers were all present. After dinner, and some lighthearted reminiscing about the past eight months we had all spent together with such a single-minded purpose, Clare spoke in a more serious vein. He thanked each one for their very special individual contribution and when he said, "Smitty-Uncle Richard, we are going to miss you driving us all over, being so patient with the kids and always maintaining your even disposition and sense of humor," he choked up. Glancing around the room I realized that all of us were sitting there with tears in our eyes. He broke it up by concluding, "and Kim, your WOW! Really put us over!" We all laughed recalling how Kim's expression had been a tension breaker many times. Clare, like most men, is not a demonstrative person given to much sentimentality, and I was happy that he was able to express his feelings so openly this evening. There's nothing like a good cry with friends followed by laughter to put you back on top of the world.

Chapter 21 Election Night

Election night we arrived at the Elks Club where family, friends, and all of those loyal workers had gathered. When they saw Clare it became bedlam. We happily circulated, greeting friends with hugs and kisses and our complete confidence began to rub off on everyone. They had been harboring some misgivings, since many had been working the area of Clare's least strength, but we knew how the rest of the district felt about the two opponents, and we never had a doubt. Busily serving a fantastic dinner to all the workers was Jack Wherry and crew, consisting of his wife Shirley, Carol and Shelly Smith, Bette Belle and Jean Smith, and Joanne Monaco, who, along with their teenagers were getting everyone fed. Shelly was acting as master-of-ceremonies, and the boys were on stage for their final and outstanding performance of the campaign.

Returns from Modesto were disappointing for Clare, but we patiently waited to hear from the hills, and Calaveras County in particular. This had been one county that Clare had not carried in the primary. It was the home of the Democrat incumbent, Senator Teal, and he had given perfunctory support to the Democrat candidate. We wanted to carry this county, big.

Friends were getting restless and nervous, so while Clare kept circulating, bolstering their flagging spirits, I stayed by the phone bank, confidently awaiting good news. When it came, there was a roar as Shelly relayed the Calaveras returns from the stage. There were several times when the vote again got too close for comfort, but it was all over, even though it took until four in the morning to get all of the results. We closed up the Elks Club at 2 a.m. and went down to headquarters to hear the last of the calls come in with Rae, Kim and the rest of the staff, some friends, the youngsters and their campaign buddies. Even Boots Warner and his gang from Amador joined us. Everyone was determined to hear the whole thing through to the finish.

As we all left for home, in a state of jubilation, albeit exhausted, the day was briefly marred by a bunch of police cars all around the street where our headquarters was situated. Two officers latched onto two of the young adults who had been with us. Not one had had anything but soft drinks all night, but their long hair or perhaps the officer's personal feelings about the election, prompted their behavior. Thank goodness Clare was there and got it settled in a few moments, and we headed for home, still happy in spite of the little show of unpleasantness.

The next day was spent happily answering the phones, accepting congratulations from so very many people near and far, who had believed in Clare ever since he had first run for office in 1969. If he hadn't lost the election in 1970, none of us might have appreciated victory quite as much, but since he had weathered defeat and had come back to win in such fine fashion, we were all walking ten feet off the ground. We heard from Willow Creek. New comers to the neighborhood had been thrown in the creeks. Clare had carried the precinct, receiving all the other five families votes. Clare was on his way, and only the future would reveal his potential, but we knew we would be proud of him...and then some.

Chapter 22: Decision Time 1976

While in the heat of the session during legislative battles, there is no time for contemplation or weighing values or discussing philosophy. It is a constant round of hard decisions that have to be made, deadlines, overlapping of committees, counting noses for necessary votes, conferences, tactics, constituents, and not enough time. There are many days of high emotional involvement in legislation, and by the end of each day, physical and emotional fatigue become apparent. When a battle is won, there is high elation, and if the prospects are not positive for the next day's battles, there is a low that takes it's toll in the legislator's overall well being.

Within the walls of the capitol there is a world of people who are steeped in the political process, with little resemblance to the real world where most of the people go about their business. Unless someone's individual rights are infringed upon, government is often ignored, taken for granted. Legislators are expected to spend much of their free time out in the district, participating in parades, counseling local agencies, giving speeches.

Family life is dearly hoarded and spent sparingly. It is a far cry from life on the farm, where the day is entirely shared by the family unit, with times of very hard work, and times of rest and relaxation, time for hunting, fishing, and travel during the week when most of the population is confined within the walls of their offices, poor devils. One of the more positive aspects of the full-time legislator's job is the fact that many of the families now live in the Sacramento area for most of the year, enrolling the children in local schools for at least half of the school year before returning to the district for the fall.

Legislative wives become active in local charities, have a Legislative Wives club that gives orientation to new members, offers bible study, social gatherings, runs a capitol blood bank for state employees, and an opportunity to share the ups and downs of the topsy-turvy world of politics. Most wives have a good working knowledge of their husband's business, and are an asset. It is a lonely life, the legislator without his family.

Perhaps the time has come when we should look to the past and see if some of the good things that were done could somehow be incorporated into the present system. The full time legislature is top heavy with members of the law profession. This does not lend itself to the basic background in a variety of experiences which would be reflected in more common sense approaches to many problems. For instance, no fault insurance is not likely to ever come out of a group of men who make a part of their living from cases of this kind. Men who have never had to meet a payroll, or run their own small business or farm, simply don't know about the problems. Not many individuals can afford to leave their businesses or profession for a number of years devoted to government service, for it is not economically possible. In the early days of the California Legislature, sessions were short and less time consuming. Granted, the times are much more complicated now than they were then, but those legislators had much more contact with the world outside Sacramento, and that is greatly needed today. There is too little communication or understanding between the public and their elected representatives and the result is a great amount of mistrust. In an address to the California Historical Society in 1949, Senator Herbert C. Jones said,

"The Legislature had been responsive to public opinion. Nevertheless, there is a popular tendency to disparage the Legislature. We make a fetish of our Courts, yet we ridicule our Legislators. When people belittle the Legislature, they reflect upon themselves, since the Legislature is simply the voice of the public."

This is mentioned in the hope that the reader may more carefully form his attitudes and opinions of his elected officials. There is a tendency by many in the public to admire the 'showhorse' Legislator rather than to appreciate those who might be categorized as 'workhorses'. The 'showhorse' is out in the district glad handing the public and showing their face at every possible public gathering. They put out press releases over everything they possibly can, initiates legislation for the sole purpose of gathering headlines, knowing full well that the legislation is never going to go anywhere. Often the public is favorably impressed by this approach. In comparison, the 'workhorse' is spending fourteen to sixteen hours a day in the capitol, working his legislation, conferring with constituents with problems that may or may not require laws to be passed, researching, consultations and phone calls. Many serious problems are solved with time and effort by the legislator and his staff without necessitating a new law. Perhaps the news media should do a bit more of investigative reporting rather than sitting back and waiting for the legislator's press releases to come rolling in. The public just might be better informed if this was the case. On the other hand, the press has been so biased in some instances that the legislators finally decided that if they wanted their story told correctly, they had better tell it themselves. Some self-discipline is needed within the field of political reporting and editorializing should be left to the editorial page. Precious time is spent writing press releases that could be better used in problem solving.

Decision time, 1976, it is. Clare decided against running for a second term. He had been a valuable 'workhorse' for the State of California, and had gained a very wonderful education in the process of serving the people who elected him. He had gladly filled in the void in San Joaquin county that occurred as a result of reapportionment, where they were left without representation for two years. Reapportionment is one of the reasons he returned to agriculture. In a sprawling district, that in the not too distant past, before the one-man-one -vote decision by the Supreme Court, was represented by seven senators and now is served by one. Here are a few statistics about Senator Berryhill's 3rd Senate District:

- The average Senate District in California contained 3,900 square miles. Clare's district had 12,000 square miles.
- The average Senate District covered 1 4/10th counties. Clare's district covered 9 counties.
- The average Senate district had 10 cities. Clare's had 23.
- The average Senate district had 350 elected officials. Clare's had 2,000.
- The average Senate district had 28 school districts. Clare's had 88.
- The average Senate district had 45 special districts. Clare's had 245.
- The typical Senate district was made up of some 500,000 persons who reside in a fairly compact area and generally share similar needs, concerns, and interests. Clare's district sprawled over mountains, valleys and in addition to the 3rd Senate district to which he was elected, he spent much time on legislative affairs for the former 6th district of San Joaquin and part of Sacramento counties, giving him almost 1,000,000 people to represent.

Reapportionment eliminated six northern counties that we had learned to love, and added tiny Mono County to the south, as well as San Joaquin and Sacramento. It eliminated a very large portion of our county of Stanislaus, and our home there. These statistics may aid the reader to get a glimpse of the enormity of the task.

Clare had always thrived on challenges and met them head-on. He carried major legislation successfully for both Governor Reagan and Governor Brown. This was in the area of state employee benefits, and a highly controversial subject to resolve. He fought to help retired persons with additional money to help off-set the tragedy of inflation, assisted local governments and small businesses. He fought hard to try and stop the possible sell out by the government to the Chavez forces in both the Farm labor Act of 1975 and the Agriculture Labor Relations Board that came as a result of that legislation. It seemed strange that when then Governor Brown called a weekend and late night meeting to iron out the details of this important piece of legislation, that he chose to not invite the one legislator who was a grape grower, and the only member of the legislature who still was active in agriculture. Those representatives of agriculture attending, being gullible went along with the Governor when he gave his word that he would appoint a fair and impartial board. The board turned out to be the people who had been deeply and ideologically involved in the Chavez social movement. The ensuing controversy, disagreement, and confusion, have born out Clare's worst fears, and we hadn't reached the negotiation stage over union contracts yet. This has been the most bitterly frustrating issue he had faced.

The last legislative session for him would be devoted in large part to correcting the inequities in the Farm labor Act, and getting a better legislative handle over the board and it's broad powers. Agriculture was still the #1 business in California, and it's important to the economic well being of the whole state cannot be underestimated. Jobs, inflation, food for the world markets as well as our own state and nation's dinner tables were affected by the outcome of this Farm Labor Act. If he was to be successful in his attempt to make necessary correction in the present, he would consider that this alone would have made the entire endeavor worthwhile. He would be able to look back at a record of solid accomplishment.

Let's look back one more time at those formative years of California's government, when the very first legislature met in 1849. When those men met in San Jose in December, it took two days for a quorum to arrive, due to rain and mud. There was no per Diem, just a lot of dedicated men from many walks of life, dedicated to helping the new state get off to a good start. They gave part of their time to government, and returned to private life to provide a living for their families. They did not have the financial burden that hangs over the candidates head today, with the exorbitant cost of campaigning. Many well intentioned candidates get themselves boxed into the position of being beholden to special interests anymore by accepting large amounts of money for campaign purposes. Clare never put up any of his own money to campaign, fully believing that is a man is a good candidate he will attract money from enough different people to support the campaign without owing any special group absolute support. This proved to be the case and he was free to vote his conscience for the four years he was in the Senate, as well as his term in the Assembly.

Our experience as a family in politics has been related to present a positive statement about the individual's opportunity and responsibility to serve. This man, Clare Berryhill, is a 'producer' of society, a man with common sense and a practical business background, with an uncommon ability to get things done. He has fought hard for what he believes and contributed a good share to good government. He looked forward to being a 'producer' again, to feel the earth, cultivate his vineyards and orchards, to be out in the fresh air. He felt that the full-time legislators, the career politicians, are not the 'producers' of society, although they perform a necessary requirement in a representative government. Unfortunately, with the advent of full-time status, the job has attracted some to it's ranks who have discovered the best job they could ever hope to have. Many would find it tough sledding indeed out in the real world. All too many are 'show horses' rather than the badly needed 'work horses'.

In conclusion, another quotation from Senator Jones speech:

"The real danger (to our State) lies in the failure of otherwise good citizens to appreciate what they enjoy under representative government. The real danger is not ideological or attacks from without ---- it is the surrender of our institutions by the indifference and inaction of Americans themselves."

"There is no royal road to good government. There is no panacea that will of itself cure the ills of democracy. Almost any form of government will work if there is a high degree of alertness on the part of the citizen, and no form will work if the citizen is apathetic. Two things are necessary on the part of the voter, if representative government is to function – an educated and unceasing interest on the part of the voters. We have to look to our schools for the first. We can only look to the individual himself to provide the second."

"The price of good government, like the price of liberty, is eternal vigilance."

'The First Legislature of California'

Address by Senator Herbert C. Jones

Published by the Senate of the State of California, 1950

Clare Berryhill participated as a citizen politician, how about you?

Clare Berryhill

From the LA Times obit:

Clare Berryhill; Former Agriculture Director and State Legislator   12/4/1925-3/18/1996

Clare Berryhill, 70, former secretary of the California Department of Agriculture and a former state legislator. Born in Fresno County, Berryhill was a grape grower in Ceres, Calif., when then-Gov. George Deukmejian tapped him in 1983 as the first Cabinet-level head of food and agriculture. During his tenure, the state was involved in combating Africanized killer bees, Japanese beetles, apple maggots, gypsy moths, Mexican fruit flies, poisoned cheeses and tainted watermelons. Berryhill served in the state Assembly in 1969 and in the state Senate in the early 1970s. He failed in a congressional bid in 1989. On Monday in Ceres, Calif., of cancer.

Clare Berryhill appeared on the front of People Magazine in an article that was written and published with People Magazine dated August 26,1985 entitled 'Clare Berryhill Defends the Golden State Against Pests and Poisons'. The article can be accessed on line via www.people.com. This article outlines some of the issues Clare dealt with while serving as Director of Food and Agriculture following his time in the California State Senate.

Maryellen Berryhill

Maryellen Berryhill, matriarch of political family, dies

Jeff Benziger
Posted: Aug. 1, 2007, 7:01 a.m.

Whether it was looking after her grape ranch, her garden or working on her paintings, Maryellen Berryhill enjoyed life. But the widow of former state Assemblyman Clare Berryhill also thrived on politics. She passed away Saturday at the age of 78.

Mrs. Berryhill's health had been failing in recent weeks as she awaited an operation to install a pacemaker. She died in a Bay Area hospital after suffering from a kidney infection.

"She was active up until the end and then peacefully died in her sleep," said Betsy Berryhill, one of Berryhill's five children.

Three members of Mrs. Berryhill's family have aspired to state office. Besides watching her husband rise to state office, she saw son Tom Berryhill elected to the state Assembly last year. Ceres School Board trustee Bill Berryhill, another son, is running for the Assembly.

Her other children are Betsy Berryhill of Camino, Jane Johnson of Sula, Mont., and Lynn Trio of Ceres.

Betsy Berryhill, an actress who appeared in New York City and Hollywood productions, said she will remember her mother as a "life so well lived. Integrity and joy and a deep spirituality that she passed on to all her kids. She lived fully and full of friends."

Assemblyman Tom Berryhill said he will remember his mother as the "consummate matriarch and backbone of our family.

"This community is truly going to miss her. She touched so many lives. Everybody loved Maryellen."

Well-known in Ceres, Maryellen Berryhill's contributions to local agriculture earned her the Agribusiness Woman of the Year award by the Ceres Chamber of Commerce in May 2003.

Born Feb. 10, 1929 to Ellen and Heine Rossel in Madera, Mrs. Berryhill grew up in Modesto and recalled wishing that her bicycle was a horse. She dreamed of farming and marrying a farmer. She did just that when she married Clare Berryhill after graduating from Modesto High School and Modesto Junior College. She went on to major in music and psychology at the University of California, Berkeley. The Berryhills married on Aug. 13, 1950, settling south of Ceres. Together they raised cattle, almonds, grapes, alfalfa, walnuts and boysenberries at their ranch at Central and Taylor roads.

Maryellen served as a music teacher for a while at Denair High School while giving private piano lessons in her home. She also supported the ranch operation any way she could and helped her kids with 4-H projects as they were growing up.

She was active in the PTA, Persephone Guild, 4-H and Republican Women.

When Clare went into politics, Maryellen shouldered more of the ranching responsibilities. Her husband was elected to the state Assembly in 1969 and later became director of Food and Agriculture for the state of California. She also helped in her husband's unsuccessful 1989 run for Congress against Gary Condit.

"She was the original political animal," said Bill Berryhill. "I miss my dad and think about him every harvest but mom I will miss her on the campaign trail. Politics was a big part of her life."

He said he remembers how his mother, a Barry Goldwater and Ronald Reagan Republican, ran Clare's political campaigns from the Ceres Dehydrator plant, which was located across the street from Richland Shopping Center.

"She did a lot of precinct work. When dad ran for the Senate, she went up and down 13 counties. She got it all organized."

After Clare Berryhill died of cancer in 1996, she split her time on the family 500-acre ranch in Sula, Montana which they established in 1995.

A supporter of the arts, Maryellen supported the Gallo Performing Arts Center in Modesto. When her daughter starred in a local theater production near Sacramento, Maryellen organized busloads of Betsy's friends and fans to go see her perform.

Because she was a "true Republican," Bill Berryhill said his mother will be buried with a necklace with the GOP elephant head on it.

Made in the USA
Las Vegas, NV
26 January 2023

66293717R00121